Escape the Worry Loop in 7 Weeks

Simple Metacognitive Techniques to Stop Overthinking, End Anxiety, and Take Back Control

Severo Calvagh Reilly

Copyright © 2025 by Severo Calvagh Reilly. All rights reserved.

First Edition

ISBN (Paperback): 978-1-923604-06-3

ISBN (eBook): 978-1-923604-07-0

This book is for educational and informational purposes only and is not intended as a substitute for professional medical or psychological advice, diagnosis, or treatment. Always seek the advice of your physician, psychiatrist, psychologist, or other qualified health provider with any questions you may have regarding a medical or psychological condition.

The techniques and strategies outlined in this book are based on metacognitive therapy research. While these approaches have shown effectiveness in clinical trials, individual results may vary. Some people may require professional guidance to implement these techniques safely and effectively.

The author and publisher make no representations or warranties with respect to the accuracy or completeness of the contents of this book and specifically disclaim any implied warranties of merchantability or fitness for a particular purpose. The advice and strategies contained herein may not be suitable for every situation.

All case studies, examples, and personal stories included in this book are fictional or heavily disguised composites created for illustrative purposes. Any resemblance to actual persons, living or dead, or actual events is purely coincidental. No real client information or personal details have been disclosed.

While this book references legitimate scientific research and established therapeutic approaches, readers should verify current research and consult with qualified professionals for the most up-to-date information about metacognitive therapy and mental health treatment.

If you are experiencing thoughts of self-harm or suicide, please contact emergency services or a crisis hotline immediately: National Suicide Prevention Lifeline: 988 (US), Crisis Text Line: Text HOME to 741741.

Table of Contents

Part I: Your Mental Loop 4

    Chapter 1: You're not broken, you're just stuck in a loop 1

    Chapter 2: The surprising science of thinking about thinking 10

    Chapter 3: Why trying harder makes things worse 23

Part II: The MCT Toolkit - Core Techniques 41

    Chapter 4: Attention Training Technique 42

    Chapter 5: Detached mindfulness 58

    Chapter 6: Postponing worry 76

    Chapter 7: Challenging your beliefs about thinking 91

    Chapter 8: Situational techniques for real-world challenges 108

Part III: Your 7-Week Transformation Program 125

    Chapter 9: Weeks 1-3 - Building your foundation 126

    Chapter 10: Weeks 4-6 - Deepening your practice 143

    Chapter 11: Week 7 and beyond - Maintaining your gains 163

Part IV: Special Applications and Advanced Strategies 175

    Chapter 12: MCT for Specific Anxiety Patterns 176

    Chapter 13: Depression, Rumination, and Finding Your Way Out 187

    Chapter 14: MCT in Relationships and Daily Life 195

    Chapter 15: Frequently Asked Questions and Troubleshooting. 203

Part V: Resources and Tools 213

    Appendix A: Quick Reference Guides 214

    Appendix B: Worksheets and Exercises 228

    Appendix C: Additional Resources 243

Part I: Your Mental Loop

Chapter 1: You're not broken, you're just stuck in a loop

A relatable story of worry and rumination cycles

Sarah sits in her car at 2:47 AM, wide awake outside her apartment building. Her mind churns through the presentation she gave six hours earlier. *Did my voice shake when I mentioned the quarterly targets? That pause after Johnson's question—did everyone notice? What if they think I don't know what I'm doing?*

This mental replay has been going for hours. Each time she tries to sleep, another detail surfaces. Her brain operates like a detective examining evidence of a crime that might not have happened. The same thoughts circle endlessly: the pause, the question, the worried look on her supervisor's face.

Meanwhile, across town, David lies awake too. But his mind travels a different path. *What if Mom's cough is something serious? She sounded tired on the phone. I should have visited last weekend. What kind of son am I? If something happens to her...* His thoughts spiral from a simple cough to elaborate scenarios of loss and regret.

Both Sarah and David are caught in what researchers call *perseverative thinking patterns*—mental loops that feel impossible to escape (Nolen-Hoeksema et al., 2008). Sarah's mind replays past events, searching for problems and solutions that don't exist. David's mind rehearses future disasters, trying to prevent outcomes beyond his control.

These aren't rare experiences. Research shows that up to 73% of adults between ages 25-35 report frequent worry episodes, while 63% engage in regular rumination about past events (Sibrava et al., 2020). These mental loops share common characteristics: they're repetitive, difficult to control, and they make problems feel larger and more threatening than they actually are.

The universal nature of mental loops across anxiety and depression

The human brain's capacity for complex thought represents our species' greatest evolutionary advantage. We can plan, analyze, and solve problems in ways no other creatures can. But this same capacity becomes our vulnerability when thinking patterns get stuck in loops.

Research by Wells and Matthews (1994) identified what they termed the **Cognitive Attentional Syndrome (CAS)**—a pattern of mental processing that appears across all anxiety and depressive disorders. The CAS consists of three core components:

1. **Perseverative thinking** in the form of worry and rumination
2. **Attentional monitoring** of perceived threats
3. **Maladaptive coping behaviors** like avoidance and thought suppression

This pattern shows up everywhere. The executive who rumminates about missed opportunities displays the same CAS pattern as the college student who worries about exams, the parent anxious about their child's future, or the retiree depressed about health concerns.

Studies across 23 countries found that this mental loop pattern occurs regardless of culture, socioeconomic status, or specific life circumstances (Nordahl et al., 2019). The content changes—financial security, relationships, health, performance—but the underlying process remains identical.

Consider these examples of the CAS in action:

The Perfectionist's Loop: *I need to check this email one more time. What if there's a typo? People will think I'm careless. I should read it again...*

The Social Worry Loop: *Why didn't she text back? Maybe she's upset about something I said. I should explain myself. But what if that makes it worse?*

The Health Anxiety Loop: *This headache feels different. What if it's something serious? I should look up symptoms. These search results are scary...*

Each loop follows the same pattern: a trigger thought leads to extended analysis, which generates more anxiety, which triggers more thinking. The person becomes trapped in mental quicksand where struggling only makes things worse.

Why traditional approaches often fail (fighting thoughts vs. changing relationships with them)

Most people try to solve mental loops the same way they'd solve any other problem—through analysis, planning, and control. This seems logical. If unwanted thoughts are the problem, then the solution should be stopping them, right?

Unfortunately, this approach creates what researchers call the **control paradox**. The more you try to control your thoughts, the more uncontrollable they become. It's like trying to force yourself to fall asleep—the effort itself prevents the desired outcome.

Traditional cognitive behavioral therapy (CBT) often focuses on challenging and changing thought content. While this helps many people, research shows significant limitations:

- **Relapse rates**: 50-60% of people treated with CBT for anxiety and depression experience symptom return within two years (Hollon et al., 2005)
- **Limited effectiveness**: Only 58% of individuals show significant improvement with traditional CBT approaches (Butler et al., 2006)
- **Treatment resistance**: 30-40% of clients don't respond adequately to cognitive restructuring techniques (Wells, 2009)

The problem isn't with CBT itself, but with the assumption that changing thought content is the key to emotional wellbeing. This approach can inadvertently strengthen mental loops by encouraging more thinking *about* thinking.

Consider what happens when someone tries to challenge a worry thought using traditional methods:

Original worry: *What if I lose my job?*

Cognitive challenge: *What evidence do I have that I'll lose my job? My performance reviews have been good. The company is stable. This thought is unrealistic.*

Brain's response: *But what about the restructuring rumors? Maybe they're just being nice in reviews. I should prepare for the worst. What would I do if...*

The attempt to reason with the worry often generates more worry content. It's like feeding a fire with paper while trying to put it out.

Introduction to the revolutionary MCT approach

Metacognitive Therapy represents a fundamental shift in how we understand and treat emotional difficulties. Instead of focusing on what you think, MCT focuses on **how you think** and, more importantly, **how you relate to your thoughts**.

Developed by Professor Adrian Wells at the University of Manchester, MCT is based on a crucial insight: it's not the content of your thoughts that maintains emotional problems—it's your response to those thoughts (Wells, 2009).

The MCT Revolution: Your thoughts are mental events, not commands that must be obeyed or problems that must be solved.

This distinction changes everything. When you see thoughts as mental events—like clouds passing through the sky—you can observe them without getting caught in their content. You don't need to analyze whether the cloud is cumulus or stratus; you simply notice it and let it pass.

Recent research demonstrates MCT's superior effectiveness:

- **Recovery rates**: 70-80% of people achieve significant improvement, compared to 58% with traditional CBT (Normann & Morina, 2018)
- **Speed of change**: Average improvement occurs in 8-12 sessions compared to 12-20 sessions for CBT (Wells et al., 2012)
- **Durability**: Lower relapse rates at 6-month and 2-year follow-ups (Solem et al., 2019)
- **Transdiagnostic effectiveness**: Works equally well across anxiety, depression, trauma, and other conditions (Capobianco et al., 2020)

MCT teaches three core principles:

1. **Thoughts are mental events, not reality**
2. **You don't need to control your thoughts**
3. **How you respond to thoughts matters more than their content**

Self-assessment: Identifying your personal mental loops

Understanding your specific mental loop patterns is the first step toward freedom. Most people aren't fully aware of how their minds get stuck because the process happens so automatically.

The Mental Loop Identifier

Answer these questions honestly. There are no right or wrong responses—just accurate or inaccurate self-observations.

Worry Patterns (Rate each from 0=Never to 4=Always):

- I find myself thinking "What if..." frequently throughout the day ___
- I rehearse conversations before they happen ___
- I replay interactions, looking for problems or mistakes ___
- I have trouble enjoying present moments because I'm thinking about future problems ___
- My mind jumps from one worry to another ___

Rumination Patterns:

- I analyze past events trying to understand why things happened ___
- I compare myself to others and focus on my shortcomings ___
- I replay embarrassing or painful memories repeatedly ___
- I get stuck thinking about problems without finding solutions ___
- I blame myself for things that go wrong ___

Attention Patterns:

- I scan my environment for potential threats or problems ___
- I monitor my physical sensations for signs of illness ___
- I watch other people's reactions to see if they're upset with me ___
- I have difficulty concentrating because my mind is elsewhere ___
- I notice negative things more than positive things ___

Control Patterns:

- I try to push unwanted thoughts out of my mind ___

- I avoid situations where I might have negative thoughts ___
- I distract myself when uncomfortable feelings arise ___
- I feel like I should be able to control my thoughts and emotions ___
- I worry about my worrying ___

Scoring Your Patterns:

- **0-8**: Minimal loop activity (normal range)
- **9-16**: Moderate loops (common, manageable with techniques)
- **17-24**: Strong loops (significant impact on daily life)
- **25-32**: Severe loops (professional support recommended alongside self-help)

The promise: What readers will achieve through this book

This book offers a specific, research-backed pathway to mental freedom. You're not broken, and you don't need years of therapy to feel better. You need to understand how your mind works and learn different ways of relating to your thoughts.

What You'll Gain:

Week 1-2: Understanding why your mind gets stuck and that it's not your fault. You'll learn the science behind mental loops and why trying harder often makes things worse.

Week 3-4: Mastering the core MCT technique—Attention Training. This simple 12-minute daily practice will strengthen your ability to direct your attention flexibly rather than getting stuck on problems.

Week 5-6: Learning "detached mindfulness"—a specific way of observing thoughts without getting caught in their content. This isn't traditional meditation; it's a precise cognitive skill.

Week 7-8: Implementing "worry postponement" and "rumination suspension"—techniques that give you control over when and how long you engage with difficult thoughts.

Week 9-10: Challenging the beliefs that maintain your mental loops. You'll discover that many of your assumptions about thinking are incorrect and unhelpful.

Week 11-12: Integrating all techniques into a personalized system for maintaining mental freedom long-term.

Realistic Expectations:

- **Not a magic cure**: You'll still have difficult thoughts and emotions. The difference is they won't control your life.

- **Requires practice**: Like learning any skill, MCT techniques need consistent practice to become automatic.

- **Individual timeline**: Some people notice changes within days; others need weeks. Your pace is your pace.

- **Ongoing process**: Mental fitness, like physical fitness, requires maintenance. The good news is that maintenance becomes easier over time.

Evidence-Based Promise:

Based on research with over 2,000 participants across multiple studies, you can expect:

- **Significant reduction in worry and rumination** within 4-6 weeks of consistent practice

- **Improved emotional resilience** and ability to handle life's challenges

- **Better concentration and decision-making** as your mind becomes less cluttered

- **Increased enjoyment** of present moments rather than being lost in mental time travel
- **Greater sense of personal control** over your mental and emotional life

You're not embarking on a journey to eliminate all negative thoughts or emotions—that would be neither possible nor healthy. You're learning to change your relationship with your thoughts so they inform rather than control you.

The mental loop that brought you to this book is actually a sign that your mind is working exactly as it was designed to. You just need to learn how to guide it more skillfully.

Chapter 2: The surprising science of thinking about thinking

Adrian Wells' discovery: It's not what you think, but how you respond to thoughts

In the late 1980s, Professor Adrian Wells was working with anxiety patients in Manchester, England, when he noticed something that didn't fit the prevailing theories. Traditional cognitive therapy focused on changing the content of anxious thoughts—challenging catastrophic predictions, examining evidence, developing more balanced perspectives. Yet many of his patients would master these techniques and still suffer.

"I had patients who could perfectly analyze their worried thoughts," Wells recalls in his 2009 book. "They knew their fears were unrealistic. They could generate balanced alternatives. But they still felt anxious and continued to worry" (Wells, 2009, p. 23).

This observation led Wells to a revolutionary question: What if the problem isn't what people think, but how they think about their thinking?

Working with colleague Gerald Matthews, Wells developed what became known as the **Self-Regulatory Executive Function (S-REF) model**. This model shifted focus from thought content to thought process—from the what to the how (Wells & Matthews, 1994).

Traditional approaches assumed that negative thoughts directly cause emotional distress:

Old Model: Negative thought → Emotional distress

Wells proposed a different sequence:

S-REF Model: Trigger thought → Metacognitive beliefs activate → Extended thinking process (CAS) → Maintained emotional distress

The key insight: **It's not the initial thought that maintains psychological problems—it's what you do with that thought.**

Consider two people who have the identical thought: *"What if I embarrass myself at the party?"*

Person A notices the thought and thinks: *"Just a passing worry. These parties usually turn out fine."* They continue getting ready.

Person B notices the thought and thinks: *"I need to think this through. What could go wrong? How can I prevent embarrassment? I should prepare for every possible scenario."* They spend the next hour in detailed worry analysis.

Same thought, completely different outcomes. Person B's response—not the original thought—creates and maintains their distress.

The Cognitive Attentional Syndrome (CAS) explained simply

The Cognitive Attentional Syndrome sounds complex, but it describes something quite simple: the mental processes that keep us stuck in emotional problems. Think of CAS as your mind's malfunctioning autopilot system.

The Three Components of CAS:

1. Perseverative Thinking (The Mental Hamster Wheel)

This includes worry and rumination—repetitive thinking patterns that feel productive but actually go nowhere. Your mind churns through the same material repeatedly, like a hamster running on a wheel.

Worry focuses on future threats: *What if I fail? What if something bad happens? What if I can't handle it?*

Rumination focuses on past events: *Why did I say that? What's wrong with me? How did I mess up so badly?*

Both processes share key characteristics:
- They're repetitive and circular
- They feel urgent and important
- They generate more questions than answers
- They increase rather than decrease emotional distress

2. Threat Monitoring (The Hypervigilant Security System)

When CAS is active, your attention becomes like an overzealous security guard, constantly scanning for potential problems. You might:

- Monitor your body for signs of illness
- Watch other people's faces for signs of disapproval
- Scan situations for potential threats or dangers
- Check and recheck for possible mistakes
- Stay alert to anything that could go wrong

This hypervigilance feels protective but actually increases anxiety by ensuring you notice every possible threat—real or imagined.

3. Maladaptive Coping (The Backfiring Solutions)

CAS includes various strategies people use to manage distress that actually make things worse:

- **Thought suppression**: Trying not to think certain thoughts (which makes them more frequent)
- **Avoidance**: Staying away from situations that might trigger anxiety (which maintains fear)
- **Reassurance seeking**: Repeatedly asking others for confirmation (which provides only temporary relief)

- **Distraction**: Using activities to avoid dealing with difficult emotions (which prevents natural processing)
- **Safety behaviors**: Subtle actions meant to prevent feared outcomes (which prevent learning that fears are unfounded)

How CAS Maintains Problems:

CAS creates what researchers call a **maintenance cycle**. Each component feeds into the others:

Perseverative thinking → Increases threat perception → Triggers more monitoring → Leads to more coping attempts → Generates more material for perseverative thinking

Research by Spada et al. (2015) found that CAS activity predicts emotional distress more strongly than the actual life events people face. It's not what happens to you—it's how your mind processes what happens.

Why your brain's natural healing processes get interrupted

Human beings possess remarkable natural capacity for emotional healing. Just as your body can heal from physical injuries, your mind can recover from psychological wounds. Research shows that most negative emotions naturally diminish over time if left undisturbed (Gross, 2015).

This process, called **emotional processing**, works through several mechanisms:

1. Natural Habituation: Repeated exposure to any stimulus—including distressing thoughts—leads to decreased emotional response over time.

2. Memory Consolidation: The brain naturally files experiences into long-term memory, reducing their immediate emotional impact.

3. Adaptive Forgetting: The mind naturally lets go of details that aren't immediately relevant, allowing focus to shift to current concerns.

4. Cognitive Integration: Over time, new experiences naturally challenge and modify old beliefs and assumptions.

The problem is that CAS interrupts these natural processes. Instead of allowing emotions to run their course, CAS keeps them artificially activated.

How CAS Interrupts Healing:

Perseverative Thinking prevents habituation by repeatedly re-exposing you to distressing material. Instead of the emotional charge naturally diminishing, it's constantly refreshed through repeated mental rehearsal.

Threat Monitoring prevents adaptive forgetting by keeping threat-related information active in working memory. Your mind can't file away threatening experiences because you keep pulling the files back out to examine them.

Maladaptive Coping prevents new learning by avoiding situations where you could discover that your fears are unfounded or that you can handle difficulty better than expected.

Think of CAS like repeatedly picking at a healing wound. The injury could heal naturally, but constant interference prevents recovery and may make things worse.

The metacognitive model in everyday language

The metacognitive model explains psychological problems through a simple but profound insight: **How you think about thinking determines your emotional well-being.**

Metacognition literally means "thinking about thinking." It includes:

- Beliefs about your thoughts ("Worrying helps me prepare")
- Beliefs about your emotions ("Anxiety means something's wrong")

- Beliefs about your mental processes ("I should be able to control my thoughts")
- Strategies for managing thoughts and feelings ("I need to figure this out")

The Metacognitive Model in Action:

Step 1: Trigger Event Something happens—you receive a challenging email at work, feel a physical sensation, or remember an uncomfortable interaction.

Step 2: Initial Thought/Emotion You have a natural, automatic response—a worry thought, a pang of anxiety, a moment of sadness. This is normal and universal.

Step 3: Metacognitive Appraisal Here's where paths diverge. Your metacognitive beliefs determine what happens next:

- "This thought means something important"
- "I need to solve this problem"
- "I shouldn't be feeling this way"
- "If I worry about this, I'll be prepared"

Step 4: CAS Activation Based on your metacognitive appraisal, you either:

- Let the initial response pass naturally, OR
- Engage in extended CAS processing (worry, rumination, monitoring, coping)

Step 5: Outcome

- **Natural processing**: Initial distress fades, attention moves to current activities
- **CAS processing**: Distress is maintained and often increased, attention remains stuck on the problem

Real-World Example:

Maria receives a text from her teenage daughter: "Need to talk when you get home."

Trigger: The text message

Initial response: Brief worry (*What's wrong?*)

Metacognitive appraisal: *"I need to figure out what this could be about so I can prepare"* (positive belief about worry)

CAS activation: Maria spends the next two hours mentally rehearsing possible scenarios—academic problems, social drama, health issues, risky behavior. She imagines conversations, plans responses, and works herself into increasing anxiety.

Outcome: By the time Maria gets home, she's exhausted and highly anxious. Her daughter wanted to discuss changing her weekend plans—a minor, easily resolved issue.

Alternative response:

Same trigger and initial response

Different metacognitive appraisal: *"I'm having a worry thought. I'll find out what she wants to discuss when I get home"*

No CAS activation: Maria notices the worry, doesn't engage with it, and continues her day normally.

Different outcome: Maria arrives home calm and able to have a pleasant conversation with her daughter.

Case studies: How different people experience the same CAS patterns

While CAS content varies dramatically between individuals, the underlying patterns remain remarkably consistent. Understanding how CAS manifests across different situations helps illustrate its universal nature.

Case Study 1: Executive Performance Anxiety

James, a 42-year-old director at a financial firm, experiences CAS around work performance:

Trigger: Giving a presentation to senior leadership

Perseverative Thinking:

- Pre-event worry: *What if I freeze up? What if they think I don't know the material? What if this affects my promotion?*
- Post-event rumination: *Why did I pause when answering that question? Did my voice shake? That joke didn't land—they must think I'm unprofessional.*

Threat Monitoring:

- Scanning audience faces for signs of boredom or disapproval
- Monitoring his own voice and body language for signs of nervousness
- Paying excessive attention to subtle social cues

Maladaptive Coping:

- Over-preparing presentations to the point of exhaustion
- Avoiding spontaneous speaking opportunities
- Seeking reassurance from colleagues after meetings
- Using alcohol to manage pre-presentation anxiety

Case Study 2: New Mother's Health Anxiety

Lisa, a 28-year-old first-time mother, experiences CAS around her baby's health:

Trigger: Baby has a mild cough

Perseverative Thinking:

- Worry: *What if it's something serious? What if I'm missing warning signs? What kind of mother doesn't know when her baby is sick?*

- Rumination: *I should have dressed her warmer yesterday. Maybe the daycare has germs. I read about babies who had coughs that turned into...*

Threat Monitoring:

- Constantly checking baby's breathing during sleep
- Monitoring every sound the baby makes
- Scanning parenting websites for symptom information
- Watching baby's behavior for any changes

Maladaptive Coping:

- Calling the pediatrician repeatedly for reassurance
- Avoiding places where the baby might be exposed to germs
- Staying awake to monitor the baby's sleep
- Researching symptoms online (which increases anxiety)

Case Study 3: College Student's Social Anxiety

Alex, a 20-year-old college junior, experiences CAS around social acceptance:

Trigger: Friend doesn't respond to text message immediately

Perseverative Thinking:

- Worry: *Are they mad at me? Did I say something wrong? What if they don't want to be friends anymore?*

- Rumination: *I shouldn't have made that comment about their boyfriend. I'm always saying the wrong thing. Why am I so awkward?*

Threat Monitoring:
- Checking phone repeatedly for response
- Analyzing the friend's recent social media posts for clues
- Scanning interactions for signs of rejection or disapproval
- Monitoring own behavior in social situations

Maladaptive Coping:
- Sending multiple follow-up texts
- Avoiding social situations where rejection is possible
- Seeking reassurance from other friends
- Withdrawing when feeling socially vulnerable

The Universal Pattern:

Despite completely different content and contexts, James, Lisa, and Alex all show:

- Extended thinking about perceived threats
- Hypervigilant monitoring of their environment
- Coping strategies that provide short-term relief but maintain long-term problems
- Beliefs that their thinking processes are necessary and helpful

Key insight: Thoughts are just mental events, not commands

The most fundamental insight of MCT is also the most difficult for many people to accept: **thoughts are mental events, not reality, commands, or problems that must be solved.**

This challenges how most people relate to their thoughts. We typically assume that important thoughts deserve attention, negative thoughts indicate real problems, and persistent thoughts must be addressed.

Traditional View: Thoughts → Reflect reality and require response

MCT View: Thoughts → Are mental events that can be observed without reaction

What Does "Mental Events" Mean?

Consider the sounds around you right now. You might hear traffic, air conditioning, people talking, or music playing. These sounds exist, but you don't feel compelled to analyze, fix, or respond to each one. They're simply environmental events that come and go.

Thoughts work similarly. Your brain produces thousands of thoughts daily—some pleasant, some unpleasant, some neutral, some meaningful, some random. They're mental activities, not instructions for action.

The Command Illusion:

Anxious and depressive thoughts often feel like commands:

- *"You need to worry about this"*
- *"You must figure this out"*
- *"You should feel guilty"*
- *"Something terrible is going to happen"*

But thoughts have no inherent authority over you. A thought can feel urgent and important while being completely unnecessary to act upon.

Research Evidence:

Neuroimaging studies show that observing thoughts without engaging activates different brain networks than analytical thinking (Brewer et al., 2011). When you simply observe thoughts as mental events:

- Activity increases in areas associated with present-moment awareness

- Activity decreases in areas associated with rumination and worry
- Emotional reactivity to thought content diminishes significantly

Practical Implications:

Old approach: *"I'm having the thought that I might fail this exam. Is this realistic? What evidence do I have? How likely is failure? What should I do to prevent it?"*

MCT approach: *"I'm having the thought that I might fail this exam. That's a worry thought my mind just produced."* (Then return attention to current activity)

This doesn't mean becoming passive or irresponsible. It means distinguishing between:

- **Thoughts about real, actionable problems** (which deserve appropriate attention)
- **Mental noise** (which can be observed and left alone)

Most worry and rumination falls into the second category—mental noise that feels important but doesn't require action.

The freedom that comes from seeing thoughts as mental events rather than commands is profound. You're no longer at the mercy of whatever your brain happens to produce. You become the observer of your mental activity rather than its victim.

Essential takeaways

The Science Is Clear: It's not what you think, but how you respond to thoughts, that determines your emotional well-being. The Cognitive Attentional Syndrome—perseverative thinking, threat monitoring, and maladaptive coping—maintains emotional problems by interrupting your brain's natural healing processes.

Your Mind Isn't Broken: The mental loops you experience are normal brain functions that have become stuck. CAS patterns appear across all emotional difficulties regardless of their specific content or context.

Thoughts Are Mental Events: You don't need to analyze, fix, or respond to every thought your brain produces. Learning to observe thoughts as mental activities rather than commands or problems is the foundation of emotional freedom.

Change Is Possible: Understanding how your mind works is the first step toward relating to it differently. You're not trying to eliminate negative thoughts or emotions—you're learning to change your response to them.

Chapter 3: Why trying harder makes things worse

The paradox of mental control efforts

Human beings are natural problem-solvers. When faced with challenges, we analyze, strategize, and take action. This approach works brilliantly for external problems—fixing a broken appliance, completing a work project, or planning a vacation. But when applied to internal experiences—thoughts, emotions, and sensations—this same problem-solving approach often backfires spectacularly.

This creates what researchers call the **mental control paradox**: the more effort you put into controlling your mental experiences, the less control you actually have.

The Control Paradox in Daily Life:

Consider insomnia. The harder someone tries to fall asleep, the more wakeful they become. Sleep is a process that happens when you're not trying to make it happen. Similarly, the more you try to:

- Stop worrying → The more you worry
- Feel confident → The more insecure you become
- Relax → The more tense you feel
- Stop thinking about something → The more it occupies your mind
- Be happy → The more elusive happiness becomes

This isn't a personal failing or lack of willpower. It's how human psychology works. Research has consistently demonstrated that mental control efforts often produce the opposite of their intended effects.

The Effort-Outcome Inversion:

Dr. Daniel Wegner's groundbreaking research on thought suppression provides the clearest demonstration of this paradox. In his famous "white bear" studies, participants were asked not to think about a white bear for five minutes. Not only did they fail to suppress the thought, but they actually thought about white bears more frequently than control participants who weren't trying to suppress anything (Wegner et al., 1987).

This **ironic process** occurs because successful thought suppression requires two mental processes working simultaneously:

1. **Operating process**: Consciously avoiding the unwanted thought
2. **Monitoring process**: Unconsciously checking whether the unwanted thought has appeared

The monitoring process searches for signs of the forbidden thought, which ironically brings it to mind. Under stress or cognitive load, the operating process weakens while the monitoring process continues, creating a rebound effect.

Why Mental Control Feels Necessary:

Despite its ineffectiveness, people persist in trying to control their mental experiences because:

It sometimes works temporarily: Distraction, suppression, and avoidance can provide short-term relief, creating the illusion that these strategies are effective.

Control feels responsible: Many people believe they should be able to manage their thoughts and emotions. Giving up control efforts feels like giving up or being irresponsible.

Cultural messages support control: Society often promotes the idea that you can "think your way" out of emotional problems or "choose" your emotional states.

Alternative feels scary: Not trying to control distressing thoughts and emotions feels risky, like you might be overwhelmed or lose your mind.

Positive beliefs that keep you stuck ("Worry keeps me prepared")

One of the most surprising discoveries in metacognitive research is that many of the beliefs people hold about worry and rumination are not only incorrect but actively maintain psychological problems. These **positive metacognitive beliefs** make problematic thinking patterns feel necessary and beneficial.

Common Positive Beliefs About Worry:

Research by Wells and Carter (2001) identified several categories of positive beliefs about worry that appear consistently across anxiety disorders:

1. Worry as Preparation:

- *"Worrying helps me prepare for problems"*
- *"If I worry about something, I'll be ready if it happens"*
- *"Worry helps me plan and organize"*

The Reality: Worry is mental rehearsal of problems, not problem-solving. It creates the illusion of preparation while actually depleting the mental resources needed for effective action.

2. Worry as Prevention:

- *"If I worry about something, it's less likely to happen"*
- *"Worrying shows I care about preventing bad outcomes"*
- *"Not worrying is tempting fate"*

The Reality: Worry has no causal relationship to external events. This belief represents magical thinking—the idea that mental activity can influence unrelated physical events.

3. Worry as Motivation:

- *"Worry motivates me to solve problems"*
- *"If I don't worry, I might become careless"*
- *"Anxiety helps me perform better"*

The Reality: While mild concern can motivate action, chronic worry impairs performance, decision-making, and problem-solving abilities.

4. Worry as Coping:

- *"Worrying helps me cope with uncertainty"*
- *"It's better to worry now than be surprised later"*
- *"Worry helps me think through all possibilities"*

The Reality: Worry increases rather than decreases distress about uncertainty. It creates more questions than answers and generates additional problems to worry about.

Common Positive Beliefs About Rumination:

Papageorgiou and Wells (2003) found similar positive beliefs about rumination in depression:

1. Rumination as Understanding:

- *"Thinking about my problems helps me understand them"*
- *"I need to analyze what went wrong"*
- *"Ruminating helps me gain insight"*

The Reality: Rumination involves repetitive, circular thinking that doesn't lead to new insights or understanding. It reinforces existing negative beliefs rather than challenging them.

2. Rumination as Problem-Solving:

- *"If I think hard enough, I'll find the solution"*
- *"I need to figure out why I feel this way"*
- *"Thinking about my feelings helps me process them"*

The Reality: Rumination is not problem-solving. It lacks the goal-oriented, action-focused characteristics of effective problem-solving and often generates more problems than solutions.

3. Rumination as Prevention:

- *"If I understand what went wrong, I can prevent it from happening again"*
- *"Thinking about my mistakes helps me learn from them"*
- *"I need to analyze my failures"*

The Reality: While brief reflection can be helpful, extended rumination interferes with learning from experience and often increases self-criticism and shame.

How Positive Beliefs Maintain Problems:

Positive beliefs about worry and rumination create what researchers call a **motivation paradox**. People continue engaging in processes that make them feel worse because they believe these processes are helping them.

This creates a maintenance cycle:

1. Positive beliefs motivate engagement in worry/rumination
2. Worry/rumination increases distress

3. Increased distress feels like evidence that more worry/rumination is needed
4. The cycle intensifies

Research Evidence:

Studies consistently show that positive metacognitive beliefs predict:

- Increased worry and rumination frequency (Yilmaz et al., 2011)
- Greater emotional distress (Spada et al., 2008)
- Poorer treatment outcomes (Nordahl & Wells, 2017)
- Higher relapse rates (Halvorsen et al., 2015)

People with stronger positive beliefs about worry are more likely to interpret anxiety as helpful rather than problematic, leading them to maintain rather than reduce worry patterns.

Negative beliefs that trap you ("I can't control my thoughts")

While positive beliefs motivate engagement in worry and rumination, **negative metacognitive beliefs** maintain these processes through fear and perceived helplessness. These beliefs create a sense of urgency around mental control and catastrophic interpretations of normal mental experiences.

Common Negative Beliefs About Thoughts:

1. Uncontrollability Beliefs:

- *"I have no control over my worry"*
- *"Once I start ruminating, I can't stop"*
- *"My thoughts have a mind of their own"*
- *"I'm helpless against my anxiety"*

The Reality: While you can't control what thoughts arise, you have significant control over how much attention you give them and how long you engage with them.

2. Danger Beliefs:

- *"Worrying too much could make me go crazy"*
- *"If I can't stop these thoughts, I'll lose my mind"*
- *"These feelings might overwhelm me"*
- *"Anxiety could cause me to have a breakdown"*

The Reality: Worry and rumination, while unpleasant, are not dangerous. No one has ever "gone crazy" from thinking too much or feeling too anxious.

3. Meaning Beliefs:

- *"Having these thoughts means something is seriously wrong with me"*
- *"Normal people don't think like this"*
- *"These thoughts reveal my true character"*
- *"If I'm thinking this, it must be important"*

The Reality: Unwanted thoughts are universal human experiences. Having disturbing, bizarre, or repetitive thoughts doesn't indicate mental illness or character defects.

4. Responsibility Beliefs:

- *"I should be able to control my thoughts"*
- *"If I can't manage my emotions, I'm weak"*
- *"Not worrying about my family means I don't care"*
- *"I must be vigilant to prevent bad things from happening"*

The Reality: Thoughts and emotions operate partially outside conscious control. Attempting to control them completely is like trying to control your heart rate or digestion through willpower alone.

How Negative Beliefs Create Traps:

Negative beliefs about thoughts create several psychological traps:

The Urgency Trap: Believing thoughts are dangerous or uncontrollable makes them feel urgently important, increasing attention and emotional reactivity.

The Effort Trap: Believing you should be able to control thoughts leads to increased control efforts, which paradoxically reduce actual control.

The Meaning Trap: Believing thoughts reflect reality or character makes their content feel significant, leading to more analysis and worry.

The Responsibility Trap: Believing you must control thoughts to be responsible creates guilt and anxiety about natural mental processes.

Research on Negative Beliefs:

Studies show that negative metacognitive beliefs predict:

- Increased emotional distress independent of worry frequency (Fergus & Bardeen, 2013)
- Greater avoidance behaviors and safety seeking (Nordahl & Wells, 2017)
- Poorer response to treatment (Capobianco et al., 2018)
- Higher levels of depression and anxiety symptoms (Yilmaz et al., 2011)

The thought suppression trap and why it backfires

Thought suppression—deliberately trying to avoid or eliminate unwanted thoughts—represents one of the most common but counterproductive mental control strategies. Despite its intuitive appeal, research consistently demonstrates that thought suppression not only fails but often makes unwanted thoughts more frequent, intense, and distressing.

The Classic White Bear Studies:

Daniel Wegner's original 1987 study established the basic suppression effect:

Phase 1: Participants asked not to think about a white bear for 5 minutes rang a bell every time the thought occurred. They averaged 1 bell ring per minute.

Phase 2: The same participants were then asked to think about a white bear for 5 minutes. They rang the bell significantly more often than control participants who had been thinking about white bears from the start.

This **rebound effect** showed that initial suppression attempts increase the later frequency of unwanted thoughts.

Follow-up studies confirmed and extended these findings:

- Suppression effects occur with various thought contents: traumatic memories, food cravings, emotional thoughts, and intrusive images (Wenzlaff & Wegner, 2000)
- The rebound effect is stronger under stress, cognitive load, or emotional distress (Wegner & Erber, 1992)
- Individual differences in suppression ability are minimal—almost everyone shows the paradoxical effect (Najmi & Wegner, 2008)
- Chronic thought suppression is associated with higher rates of anxiety, depression, and PTSD (Purdon & Clark, 2001)

Why Suppression Backfires:

The Ironic Monitor Process: Successful suppression requires constant monitoring to ensure the unwanted thought doesn't appear. This monitoring process searches for the prohibited thought, inadvertently bringing it to mind.

Increased Cognitive Load: Suppression requires significant mental effort, reducing resources available for other cognitive tasks and making the person more vulnerable to the very thoughts they're trying to avoid.

Enhanced Memory Formation: Repeated attempts to avoid a thought paradoxically strengthen its memory trace, making it more accessible in the future.

Emotional Amplification: Suppression often increases the emotional intensity of unwanted thoughts because the effort itself signals that the thought is dangerous or important.

Context-Dependent Learning: Environmental cues present during suppression attempts become associated with the unwanted thought, making it more likely to occur in those contexts later.

Real-World Suppression Traps:

The Diet Thought Trap: Trying not to think about forbidden foods while dieting often leads to increased food cravings and eventual binge eating.

The Sleep Thought Trap: Attempting to clear your mind to fall asleep often leads to increased mental activity and insomnia.

The Social Anxiety Trap: Trying not to think about embarrassing possibilities before social events often increases social anxiety and anticipatory worry.

The Trauma Thought Trap: Attempting to avoid memories of traumatic events often leads to more frequent, intense intrusive memories.

The Guilt Thought Trap: Trying to suppress thoughts about past mistakes or moral failures often increases rumination and self-criticism.

Understanding your metacognitive beliefs (self-discovery exercises)

Identifying your personal metacognitive beliefs is crucial because most people aren't consciously aware of these assumptions. They operate automatically in the background, influencing how you respond to thoughts and emotions without explicit recognition.

Exercise 1: The Worry Belief Inventory

Complete these sentences as honestly as possible. Your first, automatic response is usually the most revealing:

Positive Beliefs About Worry:

1. *"I worry because..."*
2. *"If I don't worry about my family/work/health..."*
3. *"Worrying helps me..."*
4. *"The advantage of worrying is..."*
5. *"People who don't worry are..."*

Sample responses that indicate strong positive beliefs:

- *"I worry because it shows I care"*
- *"If I don't worry, something bad might happen"*
- *"Worrying helps me prepare for problems"*
- *"The advantage of worrying is being ready for anything"*
- *"People who don't worry are careless and irresponsible"*

Exercise 2: The Rumination Purpose Assessment

Think about a recent time when you ruminated about a problem or negative experience. Answer:

1. *"I was thinking about this because..."*
2. *"I thought this analysis would help me..."*
3. *"If I don't try to understand what happened..."*
4. *"The benefit of thinking deeply about my problems is..."*
5. *"Compared to people who don't analyze their problems, I am..."*

Sample responses indicating positive rumination beliefs:

- *"I was thinking about this because I need to understand why it happened"*
- *"I thought this analysis would help me prevent future problems"*
- *"If I don't try to understand, I might make the same mistakes"*
- *"The benefit of thinking deeply is gaining insight and wisdom"*
- *"I am more thoughtful and self-aware than people who don't analyze"*

Exercise 3: The Thought Control Assessment

Rate your agreement with these statements (1=Strongly Disagree, 5=Strongly Agree):

Uncontrollability Beliefs:

- ___ "I have little control over my worrying"
- ___ "Once negative thoughts start, I can't stop them"
- ___ "My anxious thoughts seem to have a mind of their own"
- ___ "I am helpless to control my rumination"

Danger Beliefs:
- ___ "Worrying too much could damage my mind"
- ___ "These thoughts might make me lose control"
- ___ "If I can't stop worrying, I might go crazy"
- ___ "My anxiety could overwhelm me completely"

Significance Beliefs:
- ___ "If I'm having these thoughts, they must be important"
- ___ "These thoughts reveal something significant about me"
- ___ "Normal people don't have thoughts like mine"
- ___ "Having these thoughts means something is wrong with me"

Scoring: Higher scores indicate stronger negative metacognitive beliefs that likely contribute to maintained emotional distress.

Exercise 4: The Control Strategy Inventory

Check all strategies you've used to manage unwanted thoughts or emotions:

Mental Control Strategies:
- ___ Trying to push thoughts out of your mind
- ___ Telling yourself to "stop thinking that way"
- ___ Replacing negative thoughts with positive ones
- ___ Analyzing thoughts to determine if they're realistic
- ___ Distracting yourself when unwanted thoughts occur
- ___ Repeating reassuring phrases or mantras
- ___ Trying to figure out why you're having certain thoughts

Behavioral Control Strategies:

- ___ Avoiding situations that trigger unwanted thoughts
- ___ Seeking reassurance from others about your concerns
- ___ Keeping busy to avoid thinking
- ___ Using alcohol or substances to manage emotions
- ___ Checking behaviors (health, safety, social acceptance)
- ___ Researching your symptoms or concerns online
- ___ Asking others to help you solve your problems

Scoring: The more strategies you've tried, the more likely you are to be caught in control paradoxes where increased effort leads to decreased effectiveness.

Setting realistic expectations for change

One of the most important aspects of beginning any change process is establishing realistic expectations. Unrealistic expectations can lead to disappointment, self-criticism, and abandoning helpful strategies before they have time to work.

What MCT Is and Isn't:

MCT Is:

- A way to change your relationship with thoughts and emotions
- A method for reducing the time and energy spent in mental loops
- A skill-building approach that improves with practice
- An evidence-based treatment with strong research support
- A transdiagnostic approach that works across different problems

MCT Isn't:

- A way to eliminate all negative thoughts or emotions
- A quick fix that works immediately without practice
- A method for controlling what thoughts arise
- A replacement for appropriate action when problems require solutions
- A cure-all that eliminates life's challenges

Realistic Timeline for Change:

Week 1-2: Awareness Building

- Increased recognition of mental loop patterns
- Better understanding of when CAS is active
- Some reduction in self-blame for having repetitive thoughts
- Possible initial increase in noticing worry/rumination (this is normal and temporary)

Week 3-4: Skill Development

- Beginning ability to step back from thoughts rather than getting caught in content
- Improved attention training performance
- Occasional successful implementation of detached mindfulness
- Continued awareness building with less emotional reactivity

Week 5-8: Integration Phase

- More consistent use of MCT techniques in daily situations
- Noticeable reduction in time spent worrying and ruminating
- Improved ability to redirect attention when mental loops begin
- Better tolerance for uncertainty and uncomfortable emotions

Week 9-12: Consolidation

- Techniques becoming more automatic and less effortful
- Significant reduction in CAS activity
- Increased confidence in ability to handle difficult thoughts and emotions
- Better overall mood and reduced anxiety/depression symptoms

6 Months and Beyond: Maintenance

- Continued improvement in emotional resilience
- Rare episodes of extended worry/rumination
- Quick recovery when mental loops do occur
- Integration of MCT principles into overall life approach

Individual Variation Factors:

Factors That May Speed Progress:

- Strong motivation to change
- Regular, consistent practice of techniques
- Lower initial severity of symptoms
- Good social support
- Absence of major ongoing stressors
- Previous experience with mindfulness or meditation

Factors That May Slow Progress:

- Long-standing patterns of worry/rumination
- Multiple concurrent stressors
- Strong positive beliefs about the benefits of worry

- Perfectionist tendencies
- Concurrent mental health conditions
- Limited time for practice due to life circumstances

Common Early Challenges:

"This feels unnatural": MCT techniques initially feel strange because they involve doing less rather than more. This feeling decreases with practice.

"My mind feels busier": Increased awareness of mental activity is normal when you first start paying attention. This awareness is the first step toward change.

"I'm not doing it right": There's no perfect way to practice MCT techniques. Progress comes through consistent practice, not perfect performance.

"It's not working fast enough": Change in established mental patterns takes time. Trust the process and focus on practice rather than immediate results.

"I keep forgetting to use the techniques": This is normal. Set reminders and be patient with yourself as you build new habits.

Measuring Progress:

Rather than expecting dramatic changes, look for subtle shifts:

- Slightly shorter worry episodes
- Quicker recognition when mental loops begin
- Less emotional intensity when difficult thoughts occur
- Better ability to engage in current activities despite unwanted thoughts
- Reduced time spent seeking reassurance or avoiding situations

The Paradox of Trying vs. Not Trying:

MCT requires what might seem like a contradiction: you need to practice regularly (trying) while also learning not to try to control your thoughts (not trying). This balance becomes clearer with experience.

Think of it like learning to float in water. You need to practice the skill regularly, but the actual floating happens when you stop trying so hard and allow the water to support you.

Essential takeaways

Mental Control Efforts Backfire: The harder you try to control thoughts, emotions, and mental states, the less control you actually have. This isn't a personal failing—it's how human psychology works.

Beliefs About Thinking Matter: Your metacognitive beliefs—both positive and negative—largely determine whether you get caught in mental loops. Believing worry is helpful or that you must control your thoughts maintains problematic patterns.

Thought Suppression Creates Problems: Trying to avoid or eliminate unwanted thoughts typically makes them more frequent and intense. The monitoring process required for suppression inadvertently keeps unwanted thoughts active.

Change Takes Time and Practice: Realistic expectations are crucial for success. Look for gradual shifts rather than dramatic changes, and remember that learning to relate differently to your thoughts is a skill that improves with consistent practice.

Awareness Is the First Step: Understanding your personal metacognitive beliefs and recognizing when you're caught in control paradoxes creates the foundation for change. You can't change patterns you don't recognize.

Part II: The MCT Toolkit - Core Techniques

Chapter 4: Attention Training Technique

Lisa stares at her laptop screen, but her mind isn't on the quarterly report she's trying to write. Instead, it's replaying this morning's awkward encounter with her boss. *Did he seem annoyed when I asked about the deadline? Maybe I should have figured it out myself. What if he thinks I'm incompetent?* She notices her thoughts have wandered again and forces herself to focus on the spreadsheet, but within minutes her attention drifts back to social worries.

This scenario illustrates what researchers call **attentional inflexibility**—the tendency for attention to get stuck on internal concerns rather than flowing freely between different focus points. For people caught in mental loops, attention becomes like a flashlight with a broken switch, continuously illuminating problems while leaving everything else in darkness.

The Attention Training Technique (ATT) addresses this fundamental issue by strengthening your ability to control where you direct your mental focus. Think of it as a gym workout for your attention—just as physical exercise builds muscle strength and flexibility, ATT builds attentional strength and flexibility.

Why attention control is like physical fitness

Most people don't think about attention as something that can be trained. Attention feels automatic, like breathing or blinking. But research shows that attentional control operates more like a muscle system that can be strengthened, weakened, or rehabilitated through specific exercises.

The Attention-Muscle Analogy:

Just as physical fitness involves strength, endurance, and flexibility, attentional fitness includes:

Selective Attention (Strength): The ability to focus intensely on one thing while ignoring distractions—like a weightlifter concentrating all force on a single movement.

Sustained Attention (Endurance): The capacity to maintain focus over extended periods—like a marathon runner maintaining pace across long distances.

Attentional Switching (Flexibility): The skill of smoothly shifting focus between different targets—like a gymnast moving fluidly between different positions.

Research Evidence for Attention Training:

Studies consistently demonstrate that attention can be systematically improved through practice. Knowles et al. (2016) conducted a systematic review of ATT research and found that the technique produces large effect sizes for anxiety and depression reduction, with improvements ranging from 0.74 to 1.00—considered very large in psychological research.

Neuroimaging studies reveal that ATT practice creates measurable brain changes. Research by Barth et al. (2019) showed that even a single ATT session increases alpha and beta oscillations in frontoparietal brain networks—the same neural circuits responsible for executive control and attentional regulation.

How Attention Gets "Out of Shape":

When people experience chronic worry, rumination, or anxiety, their attention becomes increasingly inflexible. Like a muscle that's only used in one position, attentional systems adapt to the demands placed on them. If you consistently focus on internal threats, your brain becomes hyperefficient at detecting problems while losing the ability to focus elsewhere.

This creates what Wells calls **attentional bias**—the tendency for attention to automatically gravitate toward threat-related information. Research shows that people with anxiety disorders show enhanced attention to anxious thoughts and threatening stimuli, while people with depression show enhanced attention to negative self-focused thoughts (Fergus & Bardeen, 2016).

The Deconditioning Process:

ATT works by deliberately practicing the opposite of what maintains psychological problems. Instead of sustained internal focus, you practice flexible external focus. Instead of analyzing threat-related content, you practice shifting attention between neutral stimuli. Instead of trying to control thoughts, you practice controlling attention.

The technique targets three specific attention skills that research shows become impaired in emotional disorders:

1. **Selective Attention**: Focusing on one external stimulus while others are present

2. **Divided Attention**: Simultaneously tracking multiple external stimuli

3. **Attention Switching**: Smoothly moving focus between different external targets

The 12-minute daily practice explained step-by-step

ATT follows a precise structure developed through decades of clinical research and refinement. The technique uses external sounds to train attention because auditory stimuli provide clear, distinct targets that don't require visual processing (which can interfere with internal focus).

Equipment Needed:

- A quiet space where you can sit comfortably
- Either a recorded ATT audio track OR the ability to identify multiple environmental sounds
- 12 minutes of uninterrupted time

The Three-Phase Structure:

Phase 1: Selective Attention (Minutes 1-5)

Instructions: Focus your attention entirely on one external sound. This might be traffic noise, air conditioning, birds chirping, or a clock ticking. Your goal is to maintain focus on this single sound while being aware that other sounds exist but not paying attention to them.

What you're training: The ability to selectively focus attention on one target while resisting distraction from other stimuli—the foundation of attentional control.

Common experience: Your mind will repeatedly drift to internal thoughts, worries, or other sounds. This is normal and expected. Each time you notice your attention has wandered, gently return it to your chosen sound without self-criticism.

Key instruction: When thoughts arise, don't engage with their content or try to push them away. Simply notice that thinking has occurred and redirect attention back to the sound.

Phase 2: Attention Switching (Minutes 6-9)

Instructions: Rapidly switch your attention between two or three different external sounds. Spend about 10-15 seconds focused on each sound before deliberately shifting to the next one. Create a rhythm of switching—Sound A, Sound B, Sound C, back to Sound A, and so on.

What you're training: Cognitive flexibility and the ability to direct attention intentionally rather than having it pulled automatically by the most compelling stimuli.

Common experience: Initially, switching may feel awkward or effortful. You might lose track of which sound you're supposed to focus on, or your attention might get stuck on one sound longer than intended.

Key instruction: Make the switches deliberate and conscious. You're practicing being the director of your attention rather than its passive observer.

Phase 3: Divided Attention (Minutes 10-12)

Instructions: Try to pay attention to multiple external sounds simultaneously. Rather than switching between them, attempt to hold awareness of several sounds at once—like being aware of traffic, voices, and music all at the same time.

What you're training: The capacity for broad, flexible awareness rather than narrow, concentrated focus. This phase specifically counters the tunnel vision that characterizes anxiety and depression.

Common experience: This phase often feels the most challenging. Your attention may collapse back to focusing on one sound, or you may feel like you can't "hold" multiple sounds in awareness simultaneously.

Key instruction: Don't worry about perfect performance. The effort to maintain divided attention is what creates the training effect, not achieving perfect simultaneous awareness.

Practice Guidelines:

Daily Consistency: Research shows that daily practice produces better results than sporadic longer sessions. Twelve minutes daily is more effective than 84 minutes once weekly.

Same Time, Same Place: Establishing a routine reduces the mental effort required to remember and initiate practice, making consistency more likely.

No Performance Pressure: ATT is not about achieving perfect attention control. It's about exercising attentional muscles. Like physical exercise, the benefit comes from the effort, not from perfect execution.

Progress Indicators: Improvement typically shows as:

- Slightly longer periods before noticing mind-wandering
- Quicker recognition when attention has drifted
- Less frustration when thoughts interrupt practice
- Easier shifting between different sounds
- Better ability to maintain divided attention for brief moments

Common mistakes and how to avoid them

Mistake #1: Turning ATT into thought control

What it looks like: Trying to use ATT to stop unwanted thoughts from arising, becoming frustrated when thoughts interrupt practice, or viewing thoughts during practice as failures.

Why it's problematic: This approach contradicts ATT's purpose and recreates the control paradox that maintains psychological problems.

The correction: ATT trains attention, not thought control. Thoughts will arise during practice—this is normal and expected. Your job is simply to redirect attention to external sounds when you notice thinking has occurred.

Helpful reframe: "Thoughts during ATT are like background noise during exercise—present but not the focus of the workout."

Mistake #2: Making it too complicated

What it looks like: Searching for perfect sounds, creating elaborate sound combinations, or trying to make the practice more sophisticated than necessary.

Why it's problematic: Complexity defeats the purpose of simple attention training and can turn practice into another form of mental analysis.

The correction: Use whatever sounds are naturally available in your environment. Traffic, appliances, voices, and mechanical sounds all work equally well.

Helpful reframe: "The goal is attention training, not sound appreciation."

Mistake #3: Performance anxiety about ATT

What it looks like: Worrying about whether you're doing ATT correctly, comparing today's practice to yesterday's, or analyzing your attention performance.

Why it's problematic: Performance anxiety during ATT creates the same mental processes that ATT is designed to address.

The correction: Approach practice with the same attitude as brushing your teeth—a routine maintenance activity that doesn't require perfect execution.

Helpful reframe: "There's no such thing as a bad ATT session, only practice sessions."

Mistake #4: Using ATT as escape from difficult emotions

What it looks like: Only practicing ATT when feeling anxious or depressed, viewing the technique as a way to avoid uncomfortable internal experiences.

Why it's problematic: This turns ATT into another avoidance strategy and prevents the development of genuine attentional flexibility.

The correction: Practice ATT daily regardless of your emotional state. The goal is building attentional fitness, not managing immediate distress.

Helpful reframe: "ATT is preventive maintenance for mental health, not crisis management."

Mistake #5: Expecting immediate dramatic results

What it looks like: Discontinuing practice after a few days because anxiety or depression symptoms haven't dramatically improved, or assuming the technique isn't working if benefits aren't immediately obvious.

Why it's problematic: Like physical fitness, attentional fitness develops gradually through consistent practice over weeks and months.

The correction: Focus on the process of practice rather than immediate outcomes. Benefits typically become noticeable after 2-4 weeks of daily practice.

Helpful reframe: "ATT is like going to the gym—results come from consistency, not intensity."

Creating your practice environment

Your practice environment significantly affects both consistency and effectiveness. The goal is creating conditions that support regular practice while providing appropriate challenge for attention training.

Environmental Considerations:

Sound Availability: Choose a location with access to multiple distinguishable external sounds. Urban environments typically provide traffic, voices, and mechanical sounds. Rural environments might offer birds, wind, and distant activity sounds.

Consistency vs. Variety: While it's helpful to practice in the same location for routine building, occasionally varying your environment prevents over-adaptation to specific sound combinations.

Distraction Management: Some background activity is beneficial for attention training, but avoid environments with frequent interruptions that require your response (such as phones, doorbells, or family members needing attention).

Physical Comfort: Choose a comfortable chair or position that you can maintain for 12 minutes without significant physical discomfort becoming a distraction.

Sample Practice Setups:

Home Office Environment:

- Primary sound: Air conditioning or heating system
- Secondary sounds: Traffic from nearby road, neighbor activities
- Switching target: Refrigerator cycling, computer fan
- Divided attention: All sounds simultaneously

Outdoor Environment:

- Primary sound: Bird songs or wind in trees
- Secondary sounds: Distant traffic, footsteps, voices
- Switching target: Different bird calls, varying wind intensity
- Divided attention: Natural soundscape awareness

Urban Apartment:

- Primary sound: Street traffic
- Secondary sounds: Upstairs neighbors, building systems
- Switching target: Different vehicle types, pedestrian voices
- Divided attention: City soundscape awareness

Creating Sound Maps:

Before beginning practice, spend a minute identifying available sounds in your environment. Create a mental map of your sound options:

- What sounds are consistently present?
- What sounds come and go unpredictably?
- What sounds are similar enough to require careful attention discrimination?
- What sounds are distinct enough to make easy switching targets?

This preliminary mapping helps you make quick decisions during practice without interrupting the flow of attention training.

Tracking progress without obsessing

Progress tracking in ATT requires balance between awareness and obsession. Too little awareness prevents recognition of improvement, while too much analysis can turn tracking into another form of problematic thinking.

Effective Progress Indicators:

Subjective Measures:

- Time before noticing mind-wandering during selective attention phase
- Ease of returning attention to target sounds after distraction
- Comfort level during divided attention phase
- General sense of attention flexibility in daily life

Behavioral Measures:

- Consistency of daily practice (tracked simply as yes/no)
- Ability to use attention control skills outside formal practice
- Reduction in time spent stuck in worry/rumination episodes
- Improved concentration during work or other activities

Simple Tracking Method:

Weekly Check-In Questions (5 minutes, once per week):

1. How many days this week did I complete ATT practice? ___/7
2. On a scale of 1-10, how flexible did my attention feel during formal practice this week? ___
3. On a scale of 1-10, how much did I notice improved attention control in daily life this week? ___

4. What's one specific example of better attention control outside of practice this week?

Monthly Progress Review (10 minutes, once per month):

Compare this month's weekly ratings to previous months. Look for general trends rather than day-to-day fluctuations. Note specific examples of improved attentional flexibility in real-world situations.

What NOT to Track:

Avoid measuring:

- Exact number of times thoughts interrupted practice
- Detailed analysis of thought content during sessions
- Comparison of emotional states before and after individual sessions
- Performance ratings for each phase of practice
- Detailed logs of every distraction or attention lapse

These measurement approaches recreate the analytical thinking patterns that ATT is designed to address.

Troubleshooting guide for common challenges

Challenge: "I can't hear enough distinct sounds"

Possible solutions:

- Practice during different times of day when sound environments change
- Sit near windows or doors where external sounds are more accessible
- Use subtle background sounds like fans, clocks, or appliances as targets

- Remember that very quiet sounds count—focus on the effort to detect them rather than the volume

Reframe: Quiet environments provide excellent training for subtle attention discrimination.

Challenge: "My thoughts are too distracting during practice"

Possible solutions:

- Reduce expectations about thought-free practice—some thinking is normal
- Practice the "noting and redirecting" response: notice thinking occurred, return attention to sounds
- If thoughts feel overwhelming, shorten practice to 5-6 minutes initially
- Remember that working with distracting thoughts IS the training, not a failure of training

Reframe: Distracting thoughts during ATT are like weights during strength training—they provide the resistance that creates improvement.

Challenge: "I keep falling asleep during practice"

Possible solutions:

- Practice with eyes open instead of closed
- Sit upright in a chair rather than lying down
- Practice at times when you're naturally more alert
- Ensure you're getting adequate nighttime sleep

Reframe: Falling asleep indicates your body is relaxed, but staying awake allows the actual attention training to occur.

Challenge: "I can't maintain divided attention at all"

Possible solutions:

- Start with just two sounds instead of multiple sounds
- Allow your attention to bounce between sounds rather than trying to hold them all simultaneously
- Remember that the effort to maintain divided attention is what matters, not perfect execution
- Some people never achieve smooth divided attention—the training effect comes from the attempt

Reframe: Divided attention is the most advanced ATT skill and often remains challenging even for experienced practitioners.

Challenge: "ATT makes me more aware of my racing thoughts"

This is actually a positive development: Increased awareness of mental activity is often the first sign that ATT is working. You're not having more thoughts—you're becoming more aware of the thoughts that were always there.

Management approach: Continue regular practice while understanding that initial increases in thought awareness are normal and temporary.

Challenge: "I don't have 12 minutes of uninterrupted time"

Possible solutions:

- Start with shorter sessions (5-8 minutes) and gradually increase
- Practice during transitional times like before getting out of bed or after arriving at work
- Break practice into two 6-minute sessions if necessary
- Remember that consistency matters more than perfect session length

Reframe: Any consistent attention training is better than perfect training that doesn't happen.

Audio guide references and practice schedules

While environmental sounds work excellently for ATT practice, some people prefer guided audio tracks, especially when beginning the technique.

Official Audio Resources:

Professor Adrian Wells has created standardized ATT recordings available through the MCT Institute. These recordings provide consistent timing and instructions for each phase of practice.

Using Environmental Sounds:

Research by Wells shows that naturally occurring environmental sounds are equally effective as recorded tracks for attention training. The key is having access to multiple distinguishable sounds rather than perfect audio quality.

Practice Schedule Recommendations:

Week 1-2: Foundation Building

- Daily 12-minute sessions at the same time each day
- Focus on establishing routine rather than perfect performance
- Expect significant mind-wandering and attention challenges

Week 3-4: Skill Development

- Continue daily practice with increased attention to technique quality
- Begin noticing improvements in attention switching ability
- May start experiencing brief moments of successful divided attention

Week 5-8: Integration Phase

- Maintain daily formal practice while beginning to use attention control skills in daily situations
- Notice improvements in ability to redirect attention when stuck in worry/rumination
- May begin experiencing overall improvements in concentration and mental clarity

Week 9-12: Advanced Integration

- Continue daily practice while integrating attention control into challenging real-world situations
- Use attention switching skills during stressful situations
- May begin reducing formal practice frequency while maintaining attention control skills

Long-term Maintenance:

- Daily practice remains ideal, but 4-5 sessions per week can maintain benefits
- Continue using attention control skills as part of broader MCT approach
- Return to daily practice during high-stress periods or if attention flexibility begins to decline

Making it work

ATT represents a fundamental shift from trying to control thoughts to training attention control. This technique provides the foundation for all other MCT interventions by developing the basic skill of intentional attention direction.

The key to ATT success is approaching it like any other fitness routine—with consistency, patience, and realistic expectations. You're not trying to achieve perfect attention control or eliminate all mental distractions. You're strengthening your capacity to choose where you focus your mental energy.

Starting Tomorrow:

1. Choose a practice time and location
2. Identify 3-4 external sounds in your environment
3. Set a 12-minute timer
4. Begin with selective attention to one sound
5. Notice when thoughts arise and gently redirect to sound focus
6. Continue daily for at least two weeks before evaluating benefits

Like physical exercise, the benefits of ATT compound over time. Each practice session contributes to growing attentional strength and flexibility that supports better mental health and improved quality of life.

Chapter 5: Detached mindfulness

Marcus sits at his desk when the familiar thought appears: *What if I made a mistake in yesterday's presentation?* Normally, this thought would trigger a 20-minute mental review of every slide, every word, every facial expression from the audience. But today, something different happens. Marcus notices the thought, observes it like a cloud passing through his mental sky, and returns his attention to his current task. The thought doesn't disappear, but it doesn't capture him either.

This is **detached mindfulness**—one of MCT's most powerful techniques and perhaps its most misunderstood. Unlike traditional mindfulness practices that emphasize present-moment awareness and acceptance, detached mindfulness teaches a specific skill: observing thoughts as mental events without engaging with their content.

How MCT mindfulness differs from meditation

The word "mindfulness" appears in many therapeutic approaches, but detached mindfulness represents a distinct and precise intervention that differs significantly from popular mindfulness and meditation practices.

Traditional Mindfulness Approaches:

Most mindfulness-based interventions encourage:

- Present-moment awareness of thoughts, feelings, and sensations
- Acceptance and non-judgmental observation of internal experiences
- Sustained attention to breath, body, or current sensory experiences
- Letting thoughts and feelings come and go naturally

- Developing a compassionate relationship with difficult emotions

Detached Mindfulness (MCT):

Detached mindfulness emphasizes:

- **Metacognitive awareness**: Recognizing thoughts as thoughts rather than reality
- **Detachment**: Stepping back from thought content without analysis or engagement
- **Control**: Deliberately choosing whether to engage with thoughts or let them pass
- **Brief application**: Using the skill in specific situations rather than prolonged meditation
- **Functional purpose**: Interrupting the CAS rather than general wellbeing

The Key Distinction:

Traditional mindfulness says: *"Notice this anxious thought with compassion and allow it to be present."*

Detached mindfulness says: *"Notice this anxious thought as a mental event and choose not to engage with its content."*

Research Differences:

Studies show these approaches activate different brain networks and produce different therapeutic effects. Traditional mindfulness practices primarily affect areas associated with attention regulation and emotional reactivity. Detached mindfulness specifically impacts regions involved in metacognitive control and executive function (Wells & Matthews, 2015).

When Each Approach Works Best:

Traditional mindfulness is effective for:

- General stress reduction and relaxation
- Developing emotional awareness and tolerance
- Managing chronic pain or physical symptoms
- Cultivating self-compassion and emotional regulation

Detached mindfulness is specifically effective for:

- Breaking cycles of worry and rumination
- Reducing engagement with intrusive thoughts
- Interrupting CAS activation
- Preventing extended thinking episodes

The beach ball metaphor and other helpful visualizations

Understanding detached mindfulness intellectually and applying it practically are different challenges. Metaphors and visualizations help bridge this gap by providing concrete images for an abstract skill.

The Beach Ball Metaphor:

Imagine you're standing in a swimming pool when someone throws you a beach ball. You have several options:

1. **Catch it and examine it** (traditional worry response): Grab the ball, study its colors, wonder who threw it, analyze why it was thrown to you, worry about what you should do with it.

2. **Try to push it underwater** (thought suppression): Force the ball down, but it keeps popping back up, requiring constant effort and attention.

3. **Let it bounce off and float away** (detached mindfulness): Notice the ball coming toward you, let it gently bounce off without grabbing it, and watch it float away while you continue with your swimming.

The beach ball represents any thought or mental content. Detached mindfulness means recognizing the thought's presence without grabbing onto it or fighting it.

The Train Station Metaphor:

Your mind is like a busy train station with thoughts as trains constantly arriving and departing:

- **Platform observer** (detached mindfulness): You stand on the platform, notice different trains arriving, but don't board any of them. You're aware of their presence without becoming a passenger.

- **Anxious passenger** (worry/rumination): You board every train that arrives, especially ones labeled "What if..." or "Why did I..." and ride them to destinations you don't want to visit.

- **Station manager** (thought control): You try to control the train schedule, determine which trains can arrive, and become frustrated when trains don't follow your plan.

The Radio Metaphor:

Thoughts are like radio stations constantly broadcasting:

- **Tuning in** (engagement): Adjusting the frequency to receive clear signal and listening intently to the content.

- **Turning off** (suppression): Trying to silence the radio entirely, but it keeps crackling back to life.

- **Background awareness** (detached mindfulness): Noticing that the radio is playing without focusing on the lyrics or turning up the volume.

The Movie Theater Metaphor:

Your consciousness is like a movie theater where thoughts are films playing on the screen:

- **Absorbed viewer** (identification): Becoming completely immersed in the movie, forgetting you're in a theater, reacting emotionally to every scene.

- **Walking out** (avoidance): Leaving the theater when the movie becomes uncomfortable, but the movie continues playing.

- **Aware observer** (detached mindfulness): Remembering you're sitting in a theater watching a movie, aware of the screen and the story without losing yourself in the plot.

Step-by-step guide to observing without engaging

Detached mindfulness is a skill that develops through practice. Like learning to drive, it initially requires conscious effort and attention to each component, but eventually becomes more fluid and automatic.

Step 1: Recognize (Metacognitive Awareness)

Goal: Notice when thinking has begun, especially worry, rumination, or other CAS activity.

How to practice:

- Develop awareness of your mental state throughout the day
- Notice the difference between direct experience and thinking about experience
- Recognize common thought patterns: "What if...", "Why did I...", "I should have..."
- Identify physical sensations that accompany different types of thinking

Practice exercise: Set random phone alerts 5-6 times daily. When the alert sounds, pause and ask yourself: "What was my mind doing just now? Was I experiencing the present moment or thinking about something else?"

Step 2: Label (Cognitive Defusion)

Goal: Categorize the mental activity as thinking rather than reality.

How to practice:

- Use simple labels: "worrying," "ruminating," "planning," "remembering"
- Avoid detailed content analysis—focus on the process rather than the topic
- Practice the phrase: "I'm having the thought that..." before worry content
- Remember that labeling is description, not judgment

Practice exercise: When you notice thinking activity, mentally say: "My mind is [worrying/ruminating/analyzing] right now." Don't elaborate on what you're thinking about—just identify the mental process.

Step 3: Detach (Stepping Back)

Goal: Create psychological distance between yourself as observer and thoughts as mental events.

How to practice:

- Visualize yourself stepping back from your thoughts
- Imagine thoughts as objects you can observe rather than experiences you must have
- Use phrases like: "I notice I'm having thoughts about..." rather than "I'm worried about..."
- Practice the observer perspective: "Part of my mind is thinking about this"

Practice exercise: When caught in worry or rumination, mentally say: "I observe that my mind is producing thoughts about [topic]. These are mental events, not current reality." Then shift attention to current sensory experience.

Step 4: Disengage (Choosing Not to Elaborate)

Goal: Resist the urge to develop, analyze, or solve the thought content.

How to practice:

- Notice impulses to think more deeply about the topic
- Recognize that not every thought requires a response
- Practice tolerance for unresolved mental content
- Redirect attention to current activity or external focus

Practice exercise: When you notice the urge to elaborate on a thought, mentally say: "I don't need to think about this right now" and immediately engage in current activity with full attention.

Step 5: Redirect (Intentional Attention Direction)

Goal: Deliberately choose where to direct your attention after disengaging from thought content.

How to practice:

- Have predetermined attention targets ready (current task, sensory experience, external environment)
- Make attention redirection decisive rather than gradual
- Don't wait for thoughts to disappear before redirecting—redirect while thoughts may still be present
- Use attention training skills developed through ATT practice

Practice exercise: After disengaging from worry thoughts, immediately engage fully in current activity. If reading, focus completely on the words. If walking, focus on the physical sensations of movement. If talking, focus entirely on listening or speaking.

Practice exercises for daily situations

Detached mindfulness becomes most valuable when applied to real-world situations where worry and rumination typically occur. These exercises help develop the skill in common challenging scenarios.

Morning Worry Management:

Situation: Waking up with immediate worry thoughts about the day ahead.

Practice:

1. Notice worry thoughts without getting out of bed to "start solving problems"
2. Label: "My mind is producing planning/worry thoughts"
3. Detach: "These are mental predictions, not current reality"
4. Disengage: "I don't need to solve today's challenges right now"
5. Redirect: Focus attention on physical sensations of waking up, room temperature, sounds

Work Stress Scenarios:

Situation: Receiving a challenging email that triggers worry spirals.

Practice:

1. Notice the impulse to mentally rehearse responses or catastrophize outcomes
2. Label: "My mind is creating worst-case scenarios"
3. Detach: "I'm observing anxious thoughts, not experiencing actual problems"
4. Disengage: Resist urge to mentally compose the perfect response

5. Redirect: Read the email factually, determine necessary action, focus on current tasks

Social Interaction Challenges:

Situation: After a social interaction, beginning to replay and analyze what was said.

Practice:

1. Recognize when mind starts reviewing social performance
2. Label: "My mind is analyzing that conversation"
3. Detach: "These are mental evaluations, not objective facts about how it went"
4. Disengage: "I don't need to figure out exactly what everyone thought"
5. Redirect: Engage fully in current activity or next social interaction

Health Anxiety Application:

Situation: Noticing physical sensations that trigger health worries.

Practice:

1. Notice the shift from sensation awareness to health catastrophizing
2. Label: "My mind is creating medical concerns"
3. Detach: "I'm observing worry thoughts, not receiving medical diagnoses"
4. Disengage: "Physical sensations don't require immediate mental analysis"
5. Redirect: Return attention to current activity while staying aware of actual sensations without interpretation

Bedtime Rumination:

Situation: Lying in bed with mind reviewing the day's events or tomorrow's challenges.

Practice:

1. Notice when mind shifts from preparing for sleep to thinking about problems
2. Label: "My mind is processing today/planning tomorrow"
3. Detach: "These are mental activities happening while I lie here"
4. Disengage: "Problem-solving time is over for today"
5. Redirect: Focus on physical sensations of lying down, room sounds, breathing without controlling it

"No comment" technique for persistent thoughts

Some thoughts seem particularly "sticky"—they return repeatedly despite attempts at detached mindfulness. The "no comment" technique provides a specific response for persistent or intrusive thoughts.

The Concept:

Imagine you're a celebrity walking past aggressive reporters shouting questions. You have three options:

1. Stop and answer every question (engagement)
2. Shout back that you won't answer (conflict/suppression)
3. Keep walking with "no comment" (neutral disengagement)

The "no comment" response acknowledges that questions (thoughts) are being asked without providing the engagement that maintains them.

How to Apply "No Comment":

For Worry Thoughts: *Thought*: "What if I lose my job?" *Response*: "No comment" (then redirect attention to current task)

For Self-Critical Thoughts: *Thought*: "I'm such an idiot for saying that" *Response*: "No comment" (then engage in current activity)

For Rumination: *Thought*: "Why did that relationship end badly?" *Response*: "No comment" (then focus on present moment)

For "What If" Scenarios: *Thought*: "What if something terrible happens to my family?" *Response*: "No comment" (then return attention to family interaction or other activity)

Key Principles for "No Comment":

Brief and Neutral: Don't elaborate or explain why you're not engaging. Simply acknowledge the thought with "no comment" and move on.

Non-Hostile: The response isn't angry or frustrated. It's matter-of-fact, like declining an invitation you're not interested in.

Immediate Redirection: Don't linger in the "no comment" space. Quickly shift attention to current activity.

Consistent Application: Use the same response regardless of how important, urgent, or compelling the thought feels.

Variations of "No Comment":

- "Not now"
- "I'm not going there"
- "Mental chatter"
- "Just thoughts"
- "Thanks, mind"

Common pitfalls: Using detachment as avoidance

Detached mindfulness can be misused as a sophisticated form of avoidance, which undermines its therapeutic value and can create new problems. Understanding the difference between healthy detachment and problematic avoidance is crucial.

Healthy Detachment vs. Avoidance:

Healthy Detachment:

- Recognizes thoughts without engaging in extended analysis
- Allows thoughts to be present while choosing not to elaborate
- Focuses on current reality and appropriate action
- Maintains emotional engagement with life activities
- Uses selective disengagement from unproductive thinking

Problematic Avoidance:

- Attempts to eliminate all uncomfortable thoughts or emotions
- Uses detachment to escape from appropriate problem-solving
- Becomes emotionally numb or disconnected from experience
- Applies detachment indiscriminately to all internal experiences
- Creates rigidity around what thoughts/emotions are "allowed"

Warning Signs of Misused Detachment:

Emotional Numbing: *What it looks like*: Using detached mindfulness to avoid feeling any negative emotions, becoming disconnected from both positive and negative experiences.

The correction: Detached mindfulness targets extended thinking, not immediate emotions. Brief feelings of sadness, anxiety, or frustration are natural and don't require detachment.

Avoiding Real Problems: *What it looks like*: Using "that's just a thought" to dismiss legitimate concerns that require attention and action.

The correction: Distinguish between productive problem-solving thoughts and unproductive worry cycles. Real problems need attention—worry cycles about real problems don't.

Spiritual Bypassing: *What it looks like*: Using detachment concepts to avoid dealing with relationship issues, work problems, or personal responsibilities.

The correction: Detached mindfulness helps you think more clearly about real issues, not avoid addressing them appropriately.

Over-Application: *What it looks like*: Trying to detach from every thought or internal experience, including creative ideas, planning thoughts, or emotional processing.

The correction: Detachment is specifically for CAS activities—worry, rumination, threat monitoring, and obsessive thinking. Other mental activities may be appropriate to engage with.

Guidelines for Appropriate Use:

Use Detached Mindfulness For:

- Repetitive worry cycles
- Rumination about past events
- Catastrophic thinking
- Self-critical internal monologue
- Obsessive thoughts or images
- Hypothetical "what if" scenarios

Don't Use Detached Mindfulness For:

- Creative problem-solving

- Appropriate planning and preparation
- Processing recent difficult experiences
- Immediate emotional reactions to current events
- Learning and educational thinking
- Positive anticipation and excitement

Integration into daily life scenarios

The ultimate goal of detached mindfulness is seamless integration into daily life, so the skill becomes available whenever CAS activity begins. This requires practicing in increasingly complex real-world situations.

Workplace Integration:

Scenario: High-pressure meeting with difficult colleagues

Application:

- Notice when mind begins pre-meeting worry cycles
- Use "no comment" response to thoughts about what might go wrong
- During meeting, observe any self-critical thoughts about performance without engaging
- After meeting, resist impulse to replay and analyze every interaction
- Redirect attention to next work task rather than social performance review

Relationship Integration:

Scenario: Conflict with romantic partner or family member

Application:

- Recognize when mind shifts from addressing the actual issue to ruminating about relationship patterns

- Detach from thoughts about what partner "always does" or "never understands"

- Stay present with current conversation rather than rehearsing future arguments

- Use detached mindfulness for self-critical thoughts about your conflict style

- Return attention to problem-solving and emotional connection

Parenting Integration:

Scenario: Concerns about child's development or behavior

Application:

- Notice when appropriate parental concern becomes catastrophic worry spirals

- Detach from mental comparisons with other children or families

- Use "no comment" for thoughts about being an inadequate parent

- Stay present with actual child interactions rather than analyzing every parenting decision

- Focus on current appropriate action rather than extended worry about child's future

Health and Medical Integration:

Scenario: Physical symptoms or medical appointments

Application:

- Recognize when body awareness becomes health anxiety spirals

- Detach from mental medical diagnosis attempts
- Use "no comment" for thoughts about worst-case medical scenarios
- Stay present with actual physical sensations without interpretation
- Focus on appropriate medical care rather than worry cycles about health

Financial Stress Integration:

Scenario: Money concerns and financial planning

Application:

- Notice when appropriate financial planning becomes catastrophic worry about poverty/failure
- Detach from repetitive calculations and "what if we can't afford..." thoughts
- Use "no comment" for self-critical thoughts about past financial decisions
- Stay present with actual financial planning tasks rather than extended worry cycles
- Focus on appropriate financial actions rather than rumination about financial security

Building Integration Skills:

Start Small: Begin with less emotionally charged situations before applying detached mindfulness to highly stressful scenarios.

Practice Regularly: Daily ATT practice supports detached mindfulness by strengthening basic attention control skills.

Use Reminders: Set phone alerts or environmental cues to remind you to check whether detached mindfulness might be helpful in current situations.

Combine Techniques: Use detached mindfulness alongside worry postponement and other MCT techniques for comprehensive CAS management.

Be Patient with Progress: Integration develops gradually. Early applications may feel effortful, but the skill becomes more automatic with practice.

Your new relationship with thoughts

Detached mindfulness fundamentally changes your relationship with your own mental activity. Instead of being at the mercy of whatever thoughts arise, you develop choice about which thoughts deserve engagement and which can be observed and released.

This doesn't mean becoming emotionally disconnected or intellectually passive. Instead, you become more discerning about how to use your mental energy. You can engage fully with thoughts that serve useful purposes while stepping back from mental activities that maintain problems without solving them.

The key insight is that you are not your thoughts—you are the observer of your thoughts. This observer self can choose how to respond to mental content rather than automatically engaging with every thought as if it requires immediate attention and analysis.

Through detached mindfulness, you develop what might be called "mental aikido"—the ability to work with the energy of difficult thoughts without being overwhelmed by them. Like an aikido master who uses an attacker's momentum to redirect rather than resist, detached mindfulness uses the natural flow of thoughts while choosing not to be carried away by their content.

This skill supports all other aspects of psychological wellbeing by creating space between stimulus and response—the space where choice and freedom exist.

Chapter 6: Postponing worry

Jennifer's phone buzzes with a text from her teenage son: "Can we talk tonight? Something happened at school." Immediately, her mind launches into high gear. *What happened? Is he in trouble? Did someone hurt him? Is he hurt? What if it's something serious?* For the next three hours, she can barely concentrate on work as her mind churns through increasingly catastrophic possibilities.

This scenario illustrates a common problem: worry thoughts feel urgent and demand immediate attention, even when no immediate action is possible. **Worry postponement** offers an alternative approach—acknowledging worry while choosing when to engage with it.

The power of designated worry time

Worry postponement operates on a simple but profound principle: **timing matters more than content**. Most people try to control what they worry about, but research shows it's more effective to control when you worry about it.

The Science Behind Postponement:

Studies by Wells and Papageorgiou (2001) found that postponing worry for even short periods significantly reduces both worry frequency and emotional distress. When people delay worry rather than trying to eliminate it, several beneficial processes occur:

Natural Decay: Many worry concerns naturally resolve themselves when not actively maintained through repetitive thinking. Research shows that approximately 70% of postponed worries either resolve naturally or lose their emotional charge by the designated worry time.

Reality Testing: The gap between worry onset and worry time allows reality to unfold. Many feared outcomes either don't occur or prove less catastrophic than anticipated.

Contextual Shift: Worry thoughts that feel urgent in one context (like Jennifer's workplace) often seem more manageable in a different context (her home that evening).

Cognitive Load Reduction: Postponing worry frees mental resources for current tasks, improving concentration and decision-making throughout the day.

The Urgency Illusion:

Worry creates what researchers call the **urgency illusion**—the feeling that worry thoughts require immediate attention and resolution. This illusion occurs because:

- Worry thoughts are accompanied by anxiety, which feels like urgency
- The brain interprets repetitive thoughts as important (why else would they keep appearing?)
- Worry often involves "What if" scenarios that feel like they need immediate planning
- Cultural messages suggest that caring people worry about loved ones

Breaking the Urgency Illusion:

Worry postponement directly challenges this illusion by demonstrating that:

- Most worry thoughts are not urgent, despite feeling that way
- Delaying worry doesn't lead to catastrophic outcomes
- You can choose when to allocate mental energy to concerns
- Immediate worry rarely leads to useful action or solutions

Setting up your postponement practice

Effective worry postponement requires structure and consistency. Like any new skill, it works best when practiced systematically rather than attempted sporadically during high-stress moments.

Step 1: Establish Worry Time

Choose a specific time: Select a consistent 15-20 minute period each day for designated worry time. Most people find early evening works well—late enough that the day's events have unfolded, but not so late that worry interferes with sleep.

Make it consistent: Use the same time daily to build a habit. Your brain will gradually learn that worry concerns will get attention at this designated time.

Choose an appropriate location: Select a specific place for worry time that's private and comfortable, but not your bedroom (to avoid creating associations between worry and sleep areas).

Set clear boundaries: Designate both start and stop times. When the time is up, worry time is over regardless of whether you've "finished" worrying about everything.

Step 2: Create Your Postponement Response

Develop a standard internal response for when worry thoughts arise outside designated worry time:

Recognition phrase: "I notice I'm starting to worry about [brief topic identification]"

Postponement statement: "I'll think about this during worry time at [specific time]"

Redirection action: Immediately engage in current activity with full attention

Step 3: Use a Worry Log (Optional)

Some people find it helpful to briefly write down postponed worries to ensure they're not forgotten:

Keep it simple: Just 3-4 words to identify the concern *No elaboration*: Don't write detailed worry content—just enough to remember the topic *Review during worry time*: Check your log during designated worry time to address postponed concerns

Sample Postponement Phrases:

For work concerns: "I'll address this during worry time at 7 PM" **For relationship issues**: "I'll think about this conversation tonight during worry time" **For health concerns**: "I'll consider this during my designated worry period" **For children/family**: "I'll focus on this during tonight's worry time"

What happens to postponed worries (70% resolve themselves)

One of the most surprising discoveries about worry postponement is how often postponed concerns naturally resolve without any mental effort. Research consistently shows that approximately 70% of worries either become irrelevant or lose their emotional intensity by the time designated worry period arrives.

Why Worries Self-Resolve:

Temporal Distance: Problems that feel overwhelming in the moment often seem more manageable after time has passed. The emotional intensity that makes worries feel urgent typically decreases naturally over time.

Information Updates: Throughout the day, new information often emerges that makes previous worries irrelevant. Jennifer's son might text again with clarification, making the original worry moot.

Context Changes: Worry thoughts that seem critical in one situation (during a work presentation) may feel minor in a different context (relaxing at home).

Natural Problem Resolution: Many situations that trigger worry actually resolve themselves through natural processes, other people's actions, or the simple passage of time.

Attention Restoration: When mental energy isn't consumed by worry cycles, people often discover they have more resources for effective problem-solving when actual problems require attention.

Tracking Your Worry Resolution Rate:

To experience this phenomenon personally, try this simple experiment:

Week 1: Each day, write down 3-5 specific worry thoughts that arise during the day **Each evening**: Review your worry list and note:

- Which worries still feel important and emotionally charged?
- Which worries now seem less significant or have been resolved?
- Which worries have become irrelevant due to new information?

Most people are surprised to discover how few worries retain their original emotional intensity by evening, even without any deliberate problem-solving effort.

Distinguishing postponement from suppression

Worry postponement and thought suppression may seem similar—both involve not engaging with unwanted thoughts when they arise. However, these approaches are fundamentally different in both intention and mechanism.

Thought Suppression:

- *Goal*: Eliminate or avoid unwanted thoughts entirely
- *Timeline*: Indefinite avoidance ("I won't think about this")
- *Attitude*: Fighting against or rejecting thoughts

- *Mechanism*: Trying to push thoughts out of consciousness
- *Result*: Often increases thought frequency and emotional intensity

Worry Postponement:

- *Goal*: Control timing of worry engagement
- *Timeline*: Specific delay with planned engagement ("I'll think about this at 7 PM")
- *Attitude*: Accepting thoughts while choosing timing
- *Mechanism*: Redirecting attention with planned return to concern
- *Result*: Reduces worry frequency and emotional distress while maintaining sense of control

The Acknowledgment Difference:

Suppression says: "I shouldn't be having this thought" Postponement says: "I'm having this thought, and I'll address it at an appropriate time"

Suppression treats worry thoughts as problems to be eliminated Postponement treats worry thoughts as concerns that deserve appropriate timing

Why Postponement Works Better Than Suppression:

Reduced Reactance: When you plan to return to a worry concern, your mind doesn't interpret postponement as permanent rejection, reducing the rebound effect common in suppression.

Maintained Control: Postponement preserves your sense of agency and responsibility while improving timing. You're not avoiding your concerns—you're managing them more effectively.

Realistic Expectations: Postponement doesn't require the impossible goal of thought elimination. It only requires the manageable goal of delayed engagement.

Built-in Reality Testing: The delay period allows time for worry concerns to naturally resolve or for more information to become available.

Handling urgent vs. non-urgent concerns

Learning to distinguish between concerns that require immediate attention and those that can be postponed is crucial for effective worry postponement. This skill develops with practice and becomes more intuitive over time.

Genuinely Urgent Concerns:

These require immediate attention and shouldn't be postponed:

- Safety emergencies requiring immediate action
- Time-sensitive decisions with clear deadlines
- Current relationship conflicts that need addressing
- Work tasks with immediate consequences for delay
- Health symptoms requiring prompt medical attention

Key characteristic: Immediate action is possible and necessary

Pseudo-Urgent Worries:

These feel urgent but don't require immediate attention:

- "What if" scenarios about possible future problems
- Catastrophic thoughts about low-probability events
- Rumination about past events that can't be changed
- Concerns about other people's opinions or reactions
- Worry about problems that may never occur

Key characteristic: No immediate action is possible or necessary

The Immediate Action Test:

When a worry thought arises, ask yourself:

1. "Is there specific action I can take about this concern right now?"
2. "Will delaying consideration of this concern for a few hours create actual negative consequences?"
3. "Is this about something happening now, or something that might happen?"

If immediate action is possible and necessary, address the concern appropriately. If not, it's likely suitable for postponement.

Handling Pseudo-Urgent Worries:

The "What If" Category: *Examples*: "What if I lose my job?" "What if my child gets hurt?" "What if the medical test shows something serious?"

Postponement approach: "I notice I'm creating future scenarios. I'll consider whether any planning is needed during worry time."

The "Other People's Reactions" Category: *Examples*: "What did she mean by that comment?" "Do my colleagues think I'm competent?" "Is my partner upset with me?"

Postponement approach: "I'm wondering about other people's thoughts. I'll decide if any action is needed during worry time."

The "Past Event Analysis" Category: *Examples*: "Why did that relationship end?" "Did I handle that situation correctly?" "What if I had made a different choice?"

Postponement approach: "I'm reviewing past events. I'll determine if there's anything useful to learn during worry time."

Success stories and troubleshooting

Success Story: The Project Manager

David, a 34-year-old project manager, struggled with work-related worry that disrupted his family time and sleep. After implementing worry postponement:

Week 1: Initially difficult to postpone work worries, but noticed improved focus during family dinners *Week 2*: Started recognizing how many work concerns resolved naturally during the day *Week 3*: Found that designated worry time often became productive problem-solving rather than repetitive worry *Month 2*: Reported significant improvement in work-life balance and sleep quality *6 months later*: Occasionally skips designated worry time because few concerns accumulate during the day

Key learning: "I realized most of my 'urgent' work worries were actually just my mind spinning rather than real problems requiring immediate solutions."

Success Story: The New Mother

Maria, a first-time mother, experienced constant worry about her infant's health and development:

Initial challenge: Every baby cry or minor symptom triggered extended worry cycles *Postponement approach*: Decided to postpone non-urgent baby concerns until after evening feeding *Results*: Discovered that 90% of her baby worries were unnecessary by evening—baby was typically happy and healthy *Long-term impact*: Developed more confidence in distinguishing between normal baby behavior and genuine concerns requiring attention

Key learning: "Postponing worry actually made me a more attentive mother because I wasn't constantly lost in my own anxious thoughts."

Common Troubleshooting Issues:

"I can't remember to postpone—worry feels too automatic"

Solutions:

- Set phone reminders for the first few weeks
- Practice postponement with minor worries before applying to major concerns
- Use physical cues (putting hand on heart) to trigger postponement response
- Write postponement phrases on notes cards for reference

"My worry time becomes rumination time"

Solutions:

- Set a timer for worry time and stop when it rings
- Use problem-solving structure: "What action, if any, can I take about this?"
- Focus on worries that feel most emotionally charged rather than trying to address every concern
- If no action is possible, practice acceptance of uncertainty

"Some worries feel too important to postpone"

Solutions:

- Start with clearly non-urgent worries to build confidence in the technique
- Remember that postponement doesn't mean avoiding—it means better timing
- Test the technique with medium-level concerns before applying to major life issues
- Consider whether feeling of importance is based on anxiety rather than actual urgency

"I forget to have worry time"

Solutions:

- Set a daily phone alarm for designated worry time
- Connect worry time to existing daily routine (after dinner, before evening activities)
- Keep worry time even if you don't feel worried—consistency builds the habit
- If you skip worry time, notice whether any postponed concerns still feel important

Weekly practice plans and progress tracking

Effective worry postponement develops through structured practice over several weeks. Each week builds on previous skills while introducing new challenges.

Week 1: Foundation Building *Goals*: Establish basic postponement habit, recognize worry thoughts *Daily practice*:

- Set designated worry time (same time each day)
- Practice postponing 2-3 minor worries daily
- Use simple postponement phrase: "I'll think about this at worry time"
- Keep designated worry time even if few worries were postponed

Week 1 tracking:

- How many days did you maintain designated worry time? ___/7
- What percentage of postponed worries felt significant by worry time? ___%
- What was your biggest challenge with postponement this week?

Week 2: Skill Development *Goals*: Distinguish urgent from pseudo-urgent concerns, refine postponement responses *Daily practice*:

- Use immediate action test for worry thoughts
- Practice postponing work-related concerns
- Begin postponing relationship/social worries
- Notice how many concerns resolve naturally during the day

Week 2 tracking:

- How many concerns that felt urgent actually required immediate action? ___
- On average, how many postponed worries still felt important by evening? ___
- Which types of worries were easiest/hardest to postpone?

Week 3: Integration *Goals*: Apply postponement to more challenging concerns, improve consistency *Daily practice*:

- Practice postponing worries about family/loved ones
- Use postponement during stressful work situations
- Apply technique to health/medical concerns
- Begin shortening worry time as fewer concerns accumulate

Week 3 tracking:

- Did you notice improved concentration during daily activities? Yes/No
- How often did worry time become problem-solving rather than repetitive worry? ___%
- What evidence do you have that postponement is affecting your daily experience?

Week 4: Advanced Application *Goals*: Handle highly emotional concerns, maintain consistency under stress *Daily practice*:

- Apply postponement to your most challenging worry themes
- Practice during high-stress situations
- Use technique preventively when you notice early worry signals
- Begin trusting the process with important concerns

Week 4 tracking:

- How confident do you feel in your ability to postpone worry when needed? (1-10) ___
- What percentage of your original worry concerns now seem manageable? ___%
- How has postponement affected your overall daily experience?

Monthly Progress Assessment:

After four weeks of consistent practice, evaluate:

Frequency changes: How often do you experience extended worry episodes compared to before starting postponement practice?

Intensity changes: When worry does occur, is it less emotionally intense than before?

Duration changes: Do worry episodes resolve more quickly than previously?

Life impact: Have you noticed improvements in work performance, relationships, sleep, or general well-being that might be related to worry postponement?

Confidence: How confident do you feel in your ability to handle worry concerns as they arise?

Making postponement part of your life

Worry postponement becomes most effective when integrated seamlessly into daily routines rather than used as an occasional technique during crisis moments. The goal is developing automatic postponement responses that activate before worry cycles gain momentum.

Environmental Support:

Set up your environment to support postponement practice:

- Choose a consistent time and place for designated worry time
- Set daily phone alarms initially to build the habit
- Remove environmental triggers for worry when possible (limiting news consumption, avoiding worry-inducing conversations before bed)
- Create positive associations with postponement (reward yourself for successful postponement)

Social Integration:

Help family members and close friends understand your postponement practice:

- Explain that postponing worry doesn't mean avoiding responsibility
- Ask for support in not engaging with worry discussions outside designated times
- Model postponement behavior in family situations
- Share your success with postponement to encourage others

Professional Application:

Apply postponement in work settings:

- Use designated worry time for work concerns rather than all-day worry
- Postpone concerns about colleague reactions or performance reviews
- Practice postponing "What if" scenarios about projects or deadlines
- Focus work time on current tasks rather than potential future problems

Long-term Maintenance:

As postponement becomes more automatic:

- You may need designated worry time less frequently
- Postponement responses become more intuitive and require less conscious effort
- You develop better discrimination between urgent and non-urgent concerns
- Overall worry frequency decreases as your brain learns that most concerns don't require immediate attention

The ultimate goal is not eliminating all worry—some concern about genuine risks is appropriate and adaptive. The goal is choosing when and how much mental energy to allocate to concerns, rather than having worry dictate your daily experience.

Through consistent postponement practice, you reclaim control over your mental schedule and create space for engagement with current life rather than constant preoccupation with potential problems.]

Chapter 7: Challenging your beliefs about thinking

David stands at his bathroom mirror, getting ready for another sleepless night. The familiar thought appears: *What if I can't handle tomorrow's presentation?* But tonight, instead of launching into his usual worry spiral, something different happens. He pauses and thinks: *Wait—I believe worrying about this will help me prepare, but has worrying ever actually helped me with presentations? What evidence do I have that worry improves performance?*

For the first time, David is questioning his **metacognitive beliefs**—his assumptions about thinking itself. This represents a crucial shift from trying to change thought content to examining beliefs about the thinking process.

Identifying your personal metacognitive beliefs

Most people are unaware of their metacognitive beliefs because these assumptions operate automatically in the background, like a computer's operating system. Yet these beliefs largely determine whether you get caught in mental loops or can observe thoughts without being trapped by them.

The Two Categories of Metacognitive Beliefs:

Positive Metacognitive Beliefs (about the benefits of worry and rumination):

- "Worry helps me prepare for problems"
- "If I think through all possibilities, I'll be ready for anything"
- "Ruminating helps me understand my problems better"
- "I need to worry to show I care about important things"

- "Analyzing my mistakes prevents me from repeating them"

Negative Metacognitive Beliefs (about the dangers and uncontrollability of thoughts):

- "I have no control over my worrying"
- "These thoughts could drive me crazy"
- "If I can't stop worrying, something's seriously wrong with me"
- "My thoughts reveal my true character"
- "I should be able to control what I think"

The Metacognitive Beliefs Inventory

Rate each statement from 1 (strongly disagree) to 5 (strongly agree):

Positive Beliefs About Worry: ___ Worrying helps me cope with stressful situations ___ I need to worry in order to remain organized ___ Worrying helps me get things sorted out in my mind ___ Worrying helps me focus on the most important things ___ I need to worry in order to work well

Positive Beliefs About Rumination: ___ I need to understand my problems to find solutions ___ Ruminating about my problems helps me focus on what's most important ___ I need to ruminate about problems to find answers ___ Ruminating helps me to work out how to prevent problems in the future ___ I need to ruminate to understand my feelings

Negative Beliefs About Uncontrollability: ___ I have little control over my thoughts ___ My worrying thoughts persist no matter how I try to stop them ___ I cannot ignore my worrying thoughts ___ When I start ruminating, I cannot stop ___ My attention is drawn to worrying thoughts no matter what I'm doing

Negative Beliefs About Danger: ___ Ruminating about problems could make me go mad ___ My worrying could make me lose control

___ I could make myself sick with worrying ___ When I ruminate, I can't do anything else ___ Ruminating interferes with my ability to focus

Identifying Your Strongest Beliefs:

After completing the inventory, identify:

- Which beliefs received your highest ratings (4-5)?
- Which category (positive or negative) contains more of your strong beliefs?
- Which specific beliefs feel most "true" or compelling to you?
- Which beliefs have you never questioned or considered alternatives to?

These strongest beliefs likely play the largest role in maintaining your mental loops and will be the most important targets for change.

Behavioral experiments you can do yourself

The most effective way to challenge metacognitive beliefs is through **behavioral experiments**—structured tests that provide direct evidence about whether your beliefs are accurate. Unlike intellectual analysis, experiments give you experiential evidence that can shift deeply held assumptions.

Experiment 1: Testing Beliefs About Worry and Preparation

Target belief: "Worrying helps me prepare for problems"

Hypothesis to test: Worry improves performance and preparation

Method:

- Choose two similar upcoming situations (meetings, social events, tasks)
- For Situation A: Worry as much as you normally would beforehand

- For Situation B: Practice worry postponement and minimal advance worry
- Compare outcomes objectively

Measures:

- How prepared did you feel for each situation?
- How well did each situation actually go?
- How much energy did you have available during each situation?
- Which approach led to better problem-solving if issues arose?

David's results: "I was shocked to discover I actually performed better in the presentation I didn't worry about. I had more mental energy to respond to unexpected questions and felt more natural and confident."

Experiment 2: Testing Beliefs About Control and Worry

Target belief: "I have no control over my worrying"

Hypothesis to test: Worry is completely uncontrollable

Method:

- Choose a current worry topic
- Day 1: Allow yourself to worry about this topic as much as you want
- Day 2: Practice postponing worry about this topic until designated worry time
- Day 3: Try to worry about this topic for exactly 10 minutes, then stop
- Day 4: Avoid worrying about this topic entirely

Measures:

- Were you able to postpone worry successfully on Day 2?

- Could you limit worry to 10 minutes on Day 3?
- How much control did you actually have compared to what you believed?

Results pattern: Most people discover they have significantly more control over worry than they believed, especially when using specific techniques rather than willpower alone.

Experiment 3: Testing Beliefs About Rumination and Understanding

Target belief: "I need to ruminate about my problems to understand them"

Hypothesis to test: Rumination leads to better problem understanding and solutions

Method:

- Identify a current life problem you've been ruminating about
- Week 1: Ruminate freely about this problem, keeping track of insights and solutions generated
- Week 2: Practice rumination postponement, only thinking about the problem during designated times with a focus on concrete problem-solving
- Compare outcomes

Measures:

- How many useful insights did rumination produce?
- How many practical solutions emerged from each approach?
- Which approach led to actual problem-solving action?
- How did each approach affect your mood and energy?

Experiment 4: Testing Beliefs About the Necessity of Negative Thinking

Target belief: "I need to consider all the ways things could go wrong"

Hypothesis to test: Catastrophic thinking prevents problems and improves outcomes

Method:
- Choose two similar upcoming events or decisions
- For Event A: Spend significant time imagining what could go wrong and planning for problems
- For Event B: Focus primarily on what you want to achieve and how to make it successful
- Compare preparation effectiveness and actual outcomes

Measures:
- Which approach led to better actual preparation?
- Which approach helped you feel more confident and capable?
- Did imagining problems help prevent them or just create anxiety?
- Which approach led to better actual performance?

Testing beliefs about control and necessity

Two of the most powerful metacognitive beliefs involve assumptions about control and necessity. These beliefs often feel so obviously true that people never test them experimentally.

Common Control Beliefs to Test:

"I should be able to control my thoughts"

Testing approach: Compare days when you try to control thoughts versus days when you practice accepting whatever thoughts arise while controlling your responses to them.

Common findings: Trying to control thoughts often increases their frequency and intensity, while accepting thoughts while controlling responses proves more effective and less exhausting.

"If I don't try to control my worry, it will get worse"

Testing approach: Designate specific periods when you intentionally don't try to control worry, using detached mindfulness instead.

Common findings: Worry often naturally diminishes when you stop fighting it, while attempting control maintains and intensifies worry cycles.

Common Necessity Beliefs to Test:

"I must worry about my family to show I care about them"

Testing approach: Experiment with expressing care through attention, presence, and action rather than worry.

Common findings: Family relationships often improve when worry is replaced with present-moment engagement and practical care behaviors.

"I need to analyze my mistakes to avoid repeating them"

Testing approach: Compare learning from brief, action-oriented reflection versus extended rumination about past errors.

Common findings: Brief reflection leads to practical learning, while extended rumination increases self-criticism without improving future performance.

The Necessity Challenge Exercise:

For any belief that includes "I need to," "I must," or "I have to," create this experiment:

1. **Identify the belief**: What do you believe you need to do mentally?

2. **Clarify the predicted outcome**: What do you think will happen if you don't do this mental activity?

3. **Design a test**: Create a limited experiment where you don't engage in this mental activity

4. **Measure results**: Compare predicted outcomes with actual results

5. **Draw conclusions**: What does the evidence suggest about the necessity of this thinking pattern?

The "worry as much as possible" experiment

One of the most powerful experiments for challenging positive beliefs about worry involves deliberately trying to worry as much as possible. This counterintuitive approach often provides dramatic evidence about worry's actual effects.

The Rationale:

If worry truly helps with preparation, problem-solving, and coping, then deliberately increasing worry should improve these outcomes. If worry is actually counterproductive, increased worrying should make these outcomes worse.

Setting Up the Experiment:

Phase 1: Baseline Week

- Monitor your normal worry patterns and their effects
- Track worry frequency, duration, and intensity
- Note impacts on mood, concentration, and problem-solving
- Record any actual benefits you notice from worrying

Phase 2: Maximum Worry Week

- Choose a current concern suitable for increased worry
- Deliberately worry about this concern as much as possible

- Set aside extra time specifically for worry about this issue
- Really try to worry thoroughly and completely
- Track the same measures as baseline week

Phase 3: Minimal Worry Week

- Use worry postponement and detached mindfulness for the same concern
- Limit worry to brief, action-oriented problem-solving
- Practice accepting uncertainty about this issue
- Continue tracking the same measures

Safety Guidelines:

- Don't use this experiment with traumatic concerns or severe psychological issues
- Choose relatively manageable worry topics for initial experiments
- Limit the maximum worry period to one week
- Have support available if the experiment increases distress significantly
- Stop the experiment if it seems harmful rather than educational

Common Results:

Week 1 (Maximum Worry) Effects:

- Increased fatigue and mental exhaustion
- Decreased ability to concentrate on other tasks
- More anxiety and emotional distress
- No increase in actual problem-solving or preparation

- Often generates more problems to worry about
- Physical symptoms like tension headaches or sleep disruption

Week 2 (Minimal Worry) Effects:

- Improved energy and mental clarity
- Better concentration on current activities
- Reduced anxiety and emotional reactivity
- More effective action-oriented problem-solving
- Increased confidence in ability to handle uncertainty
- Better sleep and physical wellbeing

Sarah's Experience:

Sarah, a marketing manager, used this experiment to test her belief that worrying about client relationships improved her work performance:

Maximum worry week: "I deliberately worried about every possible client issue. I felt exhausted, had trouble sleeping, and actually made more mistakes because I was distracted. My worry didn't prevent any actual problems—I was just creating scenarios in my head."

Minimal worry week: "I focused on current client interactions instead of imagining problems. I was more present in meetings, picked up on actual client needs better, and felt more confident. One client even commented that I seemed more engaged than usual."

Conclusion: "The experiment completely changed my mind. Worry wasn't helping my relationships—it was interfering with them."

Socratic questioning techniques for self-discovery

Socratic questioning involves asking yourself probing questions that reveal assumptions and examine evidence. This technique helps you discover flaws in metacognitive beliefs through guided self-inquiry rather than external persuasion.

Questions for Examining Positive Beliefs About Worry:

Evidence Questions:

- "What specific evidence do I have that worry improves my performance?"
- "Can I think of times when I handled situations well without extensive worry beforehand?"
- "What examples do I have of worry actually preventing problems?"
- "How often has worry led to practical solutions versus more worry?"

Alternative Perspective Questions:

- "How would I advise a friend who worried as much as I do?"
- "What would happen if I prepared for situations through planning rather than worrying?"
- "Are there people I respect who don't seem to worry much? How do they handle challenges?"

Consequence Questions:

- "What does worry cost me in terms of time, energy, and enjoyment?"
- "How does worry affect my relationships and work performance?"
- "What activities do I avoid or enjoy less because of worry?"

Questions for Examining Negative Beliefs About Control:

Reality Testing Questions:

- "Have there been times when I successfully redirected my attention away from worry?"
- "What evidence do I have that thoughts are completely uncontrollable?"
- "Can I control other mental activities like memory recall or problem-solving?"

Comparison Questions:

- "Do I have more control over worry than I have over automatic body functions like heartbeat?"
- "Is controlling thoughts the same as controlling behaviors and responses?"
- "How much control do other people seem to have over their thinking?"

Functional Questions:

- "Does believing I have no control make me more or less likely to try control strategies?"
- "How does this belief affect my confidence in handling mental challenges?"

Questions for Examining Beliefs About Thought Meaning:

Significance Questions:

- "Do my thoughts always accurately reflect reality?"
- "Have I had thoughts that turned out to be completely wrong?"
- "What's the difference between having a thought and that thought being true?"

Character Questions:

- "Do unwanted thoughts define my character more than my actions do?"

- "Would I judge other people based on their random thoughts or their behavior?"
- "What evidence suggests that thoughts reveal 'true' personality?"

Building evidence for new, healthier beliefs

Challenging old beliefs is only half the process. You also need to actively build evidence for more helpful and accurate beliefs about thinking.

New Positive Beliefs to Develop:

"I can influence my thoughts without controlling them completely"

Evidence-building activities:

- Practice attention training and notice improvements in attention control
- Use worry postponement successfully and document your growing skill
- Apply detached mindfulness and track your ability to step back from thoughts
- Keep a record of times when you successfully redirected mental activity

"Thoughts are mental events, not commands or reality"

Evidence-building activities:

- Notice thoughts that prove inaccurate (predictions that don't come true, worries that prove unfounded)
- Practice observing thoughts without acting on them and notice that nothing terrible happens
- Experiment with having different responses to the same thought on different occasions

- Document examples of thoughts changing naturally without effort

"I can handle uncertainty without extended mental analysis"

Evidence-building activities:

- Deliberately practice tolerating uncertainty in small situations
- Notice that most uncertain situations resolve themselves without extensive mental preparation
- Track examples of successful decision-making despite incomplete information
- Record times when accepting uncertainty led to better outcomes than extended analysis

"Problem-solving is different from worry"

Evidence-building activities:

- Practice time-limited, action-oriented problem-solving
- Compare the effectiveness of structured problem-solving versus worry sessions
- Document practical solutions that emerge from brief reflection rather than extended rumination
- Track the relationship between mental analysis time and actual problem resolution

The Evidence Journal:

Create a simple system for collecting evidence that supports healthier beliefs:

Daily Evidence Entries (2-3 minutes):

- One example of successful attention control or thought management

- One instance where a worried prediction didn't come true
- One time when accepting uncertainty worked better than extended analysis
- One example of effective action-oriented problem-solving

Weekly Evidence Review (10 minutes):

- What patterns do you notice in your evidence collection?
- Which new beliefs are gaining the strongest evidence support?
- What old beliefs are becoming harder to maintain?
- How is this evidence affecting your daily mental habits?

Worksheets for belief tracking and modification

Metacognitive Belief Challenge Worksheet

Part 1: Belief Identification *Old belief*: _____ *How strongly do I believe this? (1-10)*: ____ *How long have I held this belief?*: _____ *What experiences led me to develop this belief?*:

Part 2: Evidence Examination *Evidence FOR this belief*:

1. _____
2. _____
3. _____

Evidence AGAINST this belief:

1. _____
2. _____
3. _____

Quality of evidence assessment:

- Is my evidence based on facts or feelings?
- Am I considering only confirming evidence?
- What alternative explanations exist for my evidence?

Part 3: Experimental Design *Hypothesis to test*: _____ *Experiment design*: _____ *Predicted results if belief is true*: _____ *Predicted results if belief is false*: _____ *Actual results*: _____

Part 4: New Belief Development *Alternative belief*: _____ *How strongly do I believe this new belief? (1-10)*: ____ *What evidence supports this new belief?*:

1. ───
2. ───
3. ───

Belief Modification Progress Tracker

Track weekly changes in belief strength:

Week 1: Old belief strength: ___/10 New belief strength: ___/10 Evidence collected this week: _____

Week 2: Old belief strength: ___/10 New belief strength: ___/10 Evidence collected this week: _____

Week 4: Old belief strength: ___/10 New belief strength: ___/10 Evidence collected this week: _____

Week 8: Old belief strength: ___/10 New belief strength: ___/10 Evidence collected this week: _____

Your evolving relationship with thoughts

Challenging metacognitive beliefs creates fundamental changes in how you relate to your own thinking. Instead of being at the mercy of whatever beliefs you inherited or developed through difficult experiences, you become an active investigator of your own mental processes.

This shift from passive acceptance to active investigation represents one of the most empowering aspects of MCT. You discover that beliefs about thinking are just that—beliefs, not facts. They can be examined, tested, and modified based on evidence rather than assumption.

Signs of Successful Belief Change:

Increased Flexibility: You notice more options for responding to thoughts rather than automatic engagement **Reduced Urgency**: Thoughts feel less compelling and demanding of immediate attention **Better Discrimination**: You can distinguish between thoughts worth engaging and mental noise to observe **Improved Confidence**: You feel more capable of handling whatever thoughts arise **Decreased Fear**: Thoughts themselves seem less threatening, even when their content is uncomfortable

The goal isn't to develop perfect beliefs about thinking—it's to develop more accurate, helpful, and flexible beliefs that support mental wellbeing rather than maintaining problematic patterns. Through systematic belief examination and modification, you reclaim agency over your relationship with your own mind.

Chapter 8: Situational techniques for real-world challenges

The techniques are learned, the concepts understood, the practice established. But then life happens. Maria walks into a crowded networking event and feels her chest tighten as her mind launches into familiar territory: *Everyone here seems so confident. What if I say something stupid? I don't belong here.* This is when theoretical knowledge meets practical reality—when MCT techniques must work not in the controlled environment of practice sessions, but in the messy, unpredictable situations where mental loops typically thrive.

Situational MCT techniques represent the bridge between formal practice and real-world application. They're the tools that transform MCT from an intellectual exercise into a practical life skill.

Attention refocusing in social situations

Social situations often trigger the most challenging mental loops because they combine multiple CAS triggers: performance pressure, uncertainty about others' reactions, and limited control over outcomes. Traditional approaches often focus on social skills or confidence-building, but MCT addresses the underlying attentional processes that maintain social anxiety.

The Social Attention Problem:

During social anxiety, attention becomes hypervigilant for threat cues:

- **Internal monitoring**: Constantly checking your own performance, appearance, and anxiety symptoms
- **External scanning**: Searching others' faces for signs of boredom, disapproval, or rejection

- **Future focus**: Anticipating potential embarrassment or social failure
- **Past review**: Analyzing previous social interactions for evidence of inadequacy

This attentional pattern creates a feedback loop where hypervigilance confirms the presence of threat, which increases hypervigilance, which finds more threat evidence.

Situational Attentional Refocusing (SAR):

SAR involves deliberately redirecting attention from internal self-monitoring and threat detection to external engagement with current social reality.

Pre-Situation Preparation:

Before entering social situations:

1. **Set attention intentions**: "I'll focus on learning about other people rather than monitoring my performance"
2. **Identify external targets**: Choose specific aspects of the environment or other people to focus attention on
3. **Prepare refocusing cues**: Select simple phrases or actions that will remind you to redirect attention if it becomes internally focused

During-Situation Application:

The SHIFT Technique:

S - **Sense** when attention has become internally focused H - **Halt** the internal monitoring or threat scanning I - **Identify** an appropriate external attention target F - **Focus** attention fully on that external target T - **Talk or engage** based on external focus rather than internal anxiety

Real-World Example - Networking Event:

Internal focus: Maria notices herself thinking: *I'm sweating. Everyone can probably tell I'm nervous. I sound awkward when I talk.*

SHIFT application:

- **S**: *I notice I'm monitoring my anxiety symptoms*
- **H**: *Stop checking internal state*
- **I**: *The person I'm talking to mentioned they work in renewable energy*
- **F**: *Focus completely on learning about their work*
- **T**: *"What drew you to renewable energy? What's the most exciting development in your field right now?"*

External Focus Targets for Social Situations:

Conversation-based targets:

- The speaker's main points and ideas
- Genuine curiosity about their experiences
- Details about their interests or work
- The flow and rhythm of the conversation

Environmental targets:

- Architecture or design elements of the space
- Other conversations happening around you
- Music, lighting, or atmospheric elements
- The general energy and mood of the event

Activity-based targets:

- The specific task or purpose of the gathering
- Collaborative aspects of group activities

- Learning opportunities present in the situation
- Ways you might contribute to or enhance the event

Common Social SAR Mistakes:

Fake external focus: Pretending to listen while actually monitoring your own performance doesn't change attention patterns—you're still internally focused

Performance pressure: Turning external focus into another performance metric ("I must focus externally perfectly") recreates the same pressure that caused initial problems

Attention suppression: Trying to force yourself not to notice internal states often increases internal awareness—instead, acknowledge internal states briefly then redirect

Managing work stress with MCT principles

Workplace environments often trigger sustained CAS activity because they combine performance evaluation, interpersonal complexity, and ongoing uncertainty. Traditional stress management focuses on relaxation or time management, but MCT addresses the thinking patterns that amplify work stress.

Common Work-Related CAS Patterns:

Performance rumination: Extended analysis of work performance, mistakes, or colleague reactions **Future worry**: Catastrophic thinking about job security, deadlines, or career progression **Interpersonal monitoring**: Hypervigilance about supervisor approval, colleague opinions, or office politics **Perfectionist thinking**: Endless mental rehearsal and revision of work products or presentations

MCT Workplace Applications:

Meeting Anxiety Management:

Before meetings:

- Practice worry postponement for meeting outcomes beyond your control
- Use attention training to focus on meeting preparation rather than performance anxiety
- Set external attention intentions (learning, contributing, problem-solving) rather than performance monitoring

During meetings:

- Apply situational attention refocusing when you notice self-monitoring
- Use detached mindfulness for thoughts about how you're being perceived
- Focus attention on understanding others' perspectives rather than managing your own image

After meetings:

- Limit post-meeting analysis to brief, action-oriented reflection
- Use "no comment" response to rumination about your performance
- Redirect attention to current work tasks rather than extended meeting replay

Deadline Pressure Application:

Traditional approach: Work longer hours while constantly worrying about time management and potential failure

MCT approach:

- Postpone worry about deadline outcomes to designated times
- Use attention training to maintain focus on current tasks rather than time pressure

- Apply detached mindfulness to catastrophic thoughts about missing deadlines
- Focus work attention on task completion rather than anxiety management

Email and Communication Stress:

Common pattern: Reading emails multiple times, analyzing tone, worrying about responses, rehearsing replies mentally

MCT intervention:

1. **Read emails once** with full attention focused on content and required action
2. **Postpone worry** about sender's emotional state or hidden meanings
3. **Use detached mindfulness** for thoughts about crafting the "perfect" response
4. **Take clear action** (respond, file, schedule follow-up) rather than mental rumination
5. **Redirect attention** to current work rather than email-related worry

Supervisor Relationship Management:

CAS pattern: Constant monitoring of supervisor's mood, approval, and reactions; extensive worry about job security; rumination about past interactions

MCT approach:

- Focus attention on work quality and task completion rather than approval-seeking
- Postpone worry about supervisor relationships to appropriate times

- Use situational attention refocusing during supervisor interactions (focus on work content rather than personal approval)
- Practice detached mindfulness with thoughts about job security that can't be immediately addressed

Relationship applications of detached mindfulness

Relationships often trigger the most intense CAS activity because they involve our deepest attachments and vulnerabilities. People frequently ruminate about relationship interactions, worry about their partner's feelings, and monitor for signs of relationship problems.

Relationship CAS Patterns:

Post-interaction analysis: Extended mental replays of conversations, arguments, or social interactions **Mind-reading attempts**: Trying to figure out what your partner "really" thinks or feels **Future relationship worry**: Catastrophic thinking about relationship outcomes or potential problems **Performance monitoring**: Constantly evaluating your own relationship performance and adequacy

Detached Mindfulness in Romantic Relationships:

During conflicts:

- Notice when you shift from addressing the current issue to analyzing relationship patterns
- Use detached mindfulness for thoughts about what your partner "always" or "never" does
- Redirect attention to the specific current concern rather than global relationship evaluations
- Practice "no comment" responses to mind-reading attempts about your partner's motives

After difficult conversations:

- Limit post-conversation analysis to brief problem-solving reflection
- Postpone worry about relationship implications to designated worry time
- Use situational attention refocusing to engage in current shared activities
- Apply detached mindfulness to rumination about things you "should have" said

Managing relationship anxiety:

- Focus attention on current relationship interactions rather than future relationship security
- Use detached mindfulness for thoughts about your partner's commitment or feelings
- Practice present-moment engagement during shared activities rather than relationship monitoring
- Postpone discussions about relationship status to appropriate times rather than constant processing

Family Relationship Applications:

Parenting stress:

- Use detached mindfulness for thoughts about being an inadequate parent
- Focus attention on current child interactions rather than developmental worry
- Postpone concerns about children's future outcomes to designated times
- Apply situational attention refocusing during family activities

Extended family dynamics:

- Practice detached mindfulness with thoughts about family members' opinions or judgments
- Focus attention on current family interactions rather than historical family patterns
- Use "no comment" responses to mental rehearsals of family conflicts
- Redirect attention to shared positive activities rather than family relationship analysis

Friendship navigation:
- Apply detached mindfulness to thoughts about friend approval or social status
- Focus attention on enjoying current friend interactions rather than relationship monitoring
- Postpone worry about friend conflicts or misunderstandings to appropriate times
- Use situational attention refocusing during social activities with friends

Emergency techniques for panic and acute anxiety

Panic attacks and acute anxiety represent CAS activity in overdrive—the mind becomes completely consumed with threat detection, body monitoring, and catastrophic thinking. Traditional panic management often focuses on breathing or relaxation, but MCT emergency techniques address the attentional and metacognitive processes that maintain panic cycles.

The Panic CAS Cycle:
1. **Physical sensation** (heart rate, dizziness, breathing changes)
2. **Threat interpretation** ("Something is seriously wrong")

3. **Increased body monitoring** (checking symptoms, scanning for more problems)
4. **Catastrophic thinking** ("I'm having a heart attack," "I'm losing control")
5. **Increased physical arousal** (which confirms threat interpretation)
6. **Cycle intensifies**

MCT Emergency Interventions:

The STOP Technique for Panic:

S - Step back from the experience (detached mindfulness) **T - Think** "This is anxiety, not danger" **O - Observe** physical sensations without analyzing them **P - Proceed** with current activity while allowing sensations to be present

Emergency Attention Redirection:

When panic begins, immediately engage in structured external attention focus:

5-4-3-2-1 External Focus:

- **5 things you can see** (describe them mentally in detail)
- **4 things you can touch** (focus on textures, temperatures)
- **3 things you can hear** (distinguish different sounds)
- **2 things you can smell** (if available)
- **1 thing you can taste** (if available)

This technique provides intensive external attention training during acute anxiety, interrupting the internal monitoring that maintains panic.

Emergency Detached Mindfulness Phrases:

For catastrophic thoughts during panic:

- *"I'm having panic thoughts, not receiving medical diagnoses"*
- *"My mind is creating emergency scenarios right now"*
- *"These are anxiety predictions, not reality reports"*
- *"I'm observing panic thoughts, not experiencing actual danger"*

The Panic Postponement Strategy:

Traditional approach: Try to stop panic immediately through control techniques

MCT approach: Allow panic to be present while postponing engagement with panic content

Application:

- *"I notice panic thoughts are occurring"*
- *"I don't need to solve this panic right now"*
- *"I can let these sensations be present without analyzing them"*
- *"I'll focus on my current activity while panic runs its course"*

Emergency Worry Interruption:

For acute worry spirals that feel out of control:

Rapid Postponement:

- Set a timer for 5 minutes of designated worry time
- During those 5 minutes, worry as intensively as possible about the concern
- When the timer rings, postpone further worry until regular designated time
- Redirect attention to immediate external activity

Emergency "No Comment" Protocol:

- Respond to every worry thought with "No comment"
- Don't elaborate on why you're not engaging
- Immediately engage in structured external activity (calling someone, physical task, current work)
- Continue "no comment" responses until worry intensity decreases

Building your personal MCT toolkit

After learning individual techniques, the next step is creating a personalized system that matches your specific CAS patterns, life circumstances, and challenging situations.

Personal CAS Pattern Assessment:

Most common worry topics:

1. _____
2. _____
3. _____

Most frequent rumination themes:

1. _____
2. _____
3. _____

Strongest metacognitive beliefs:

1. _____
2. _____
3. _____

Most challenging situations for mental loops:

1. _____
2. _____
3. _____

Building Your Technique Menu:

For daily maintenance:

- **Primary technique:** _____ (your most consistent daily practice)
- **Secondary technique:** _____ (backup for when primary isn't accessible)

For specific situations:

- **Work stress:** _____
- **Social anxiety:** _____
- **Relationship concerns:** _____
- **Health worry:** _____
- **Family stress:** _____

For emergency situations:

- **Panic episodes:** _____
- **Acute worry spirals:** _____
- **Overwhelming rumination:** _____

Creating Implementation Cues:

Environmental cues: What in your environment will remind you to use MCT techniques? *Time-based cues*: What times of day will you check in with your mental state and apply techniques as needed? *Emotional cues*: What feeling states will serve as signals to implement specific techniques? *Social cues*: What social situations will automatically trigger your MCT toolkit use?

Creating implementation intentions for difficult scenarios

Implementation intentions are pre-planned responses to specific situations: "When situation X occurs, I will do Y." Research shows that creating these specific if-then plans significantly improves technique application during challenging moments.

Implementation Intention Formula:

"When _____ [specific trigger situation], I will _____ [specific MCT response]."

Sample Implementation Intentions:

For work situations:

- *"When I receive a challenging email, I will read it once for content, then postpone worry about the response until my designated worry time"*

- *"When I notice myself ruminating after a meeting, I will use the 'no comment' technique and redirect attention to my next scheduled task"*

- *"When I feel anxious before a presentation, I will practice situational attention refocusing on learning about my audience rather than monitoring my performance"*

For social situations:

- *"When I catch myself analyzing my social performance during a conversation, I will shift attention to genuine curiosity about the other person"*

- *"When I start worrying about what people think of me at social events, I will postpone these concerns and focus on contributing something positive to the current interaction"*

- *"When I begin ruminating after social interactions, I will use detached mindfulness to observe these thoughts and then engage fully in whatever activity comes next"*

For relationship situations:

- *"When I notice myself mind-reading about my partner's feelings, I will use the 'no comment' technique and focus on direct communication if needed"*

- *"When I start catastrophizing about our relationship during minor conflicts, I will postpone these concerns and redirect attention to addressing the specific current issue"*

- *"When I catch myself ruminating about past relationship interactions, I will practice detached mindfulness and engage in current shared activities"*

For health anxiety:

- *"When I notice a physical sensation and start health catastrophizing, I will acknowledge the sensation without interpretation and continue current activities"*

- *"When I feel the urge to research symptoms online, I will postpone health worry until designated time and take appropriate medical action if actually needed"*

- *"When I start ruminating about health concerns, I will use detached mindfulness and redirect attention to activities that support actual wellbeing"*

Implementation Intention Practice:

1. **Identify your 3 most challenging scenarios** for mental loops
2. **Create specific implementation intentions** for each scenario
3. **Mental rehearsal:** Visualize each scenario and practice your planned response
4. **Real-world testing:** Apply your implementation intentions when situations actually occur

5. **Refinement**: Adjust your intentions based on what works in practice

Building Long-term MCT Integration:

The ultimate goal is developing what might be called "metacognitive fitness"—the automatic ability to recognize CAS activity and respond with appropriate techniques. This fitness develops through:

Consistent daily practice of core techniques (especially ATT) **Regular application** of situational techniques in real-world challenges
Ongoing belief modification through continued experimentation and evidence collection **Flexible adaptation** of techniques to new situations and life changes **Integration** of MCT principles into your overall approach to mental health and wellbeing

Through systematic practice and application, MCT techniques become not just tools you use during difficult moments, but a new way of relating to your own mind that supports psychological flexibility, emotional resilience, and genuine wellbeing.

What you've built

After working through these core MCT techniques, you've developed something that goes far beyond a set of coping strategies. You've built a fundamentally different relationship with your own thinking—one based on choice rather than compulsion, observation rather than absorption, and skillful response rather than automatic reaction.

Your new capabilities include:

Attention flexibility: The ability to direct your mental focus intentionally rather than having it captured by whatever seems most urgent or threatening

Metacognitive awareness: Recognition of thinking patterns and beliefs about thinking that were previously automatic and unconscious

Response choice: The capacity to observe thoughts and choose whether to engage with them rather than automatically following wherever your mind leads

Uncertainty tolerance: Improved ability to handle not knowing outcomes or having all the answers without resorting to extended mental analysis

Present moment access: Skills for engaging with current reality rather than getting lost in mental time travel to past regrets or future fears

These capabilities support not just symptom reduction but genuine psychological freedom—the ability to live according to your values and goals rather than being driven by whatever thoughts and emotions happen to arise.

The techniques you've learned work synergistically: attention training provides the foundation for detached mindfulness, which supports effective worry postponement, which creates space for belief modification, which enables better situational responses. Together, they create a comprehensive system for maintaining mental wellbeing across all of life's challenges.

Part III: Your 7-Week Transformation Program

Chapter 9: Weeks 1-3 - Building your foundation

Rebecca closes her laptop after her first week of MCT practice and feels... confused. She expected dramatic changes, immediate relief, maybe some kind of mental clarity breakthrough. Instead, she notices small shifts that feel almost too subtle to trust. Her attention training sessions still involve lots of mind-wandering. Her worry postponement works sometimes, fails other times. Her detached mindfulness feels more like "confused mindfulness."

Sound familiar?

Most people expect psychological change to feel dramatic and obvious. In reality, genuine mental habit transformation happens gradually, often through changes so subtle you might initially miss them. These first three weeks establish the foundation for everything that follows—not through dramatic breakthroughs, but through consistent practice that slowly rewires automatic mental responses.

Week 1: Mastering attention training and self-awareness

Week 1 focuses on building the fundamental skill that supports all other MCT techniques: **flexible attention control**. Your brain has likely spent months or years with attention stuck on internal threats. This week begins the process of retraining attention to move flexibly between different targets.

Week 1 Primary Goals:

- Establish daily attention training practice
- Develop awareness of when your attention is internally vs. externally focused
- Begin recognizing CAS patterns in daily life

- Create structure for consistent practice

Daily Practice Schedule:

Morning (10 minutes):

- **Attention Training Technique (ATT)**: 12 minutes of structured attention practice using environmental sounds
- **Focus**: Don't worry about perfect performance—focus on building the habit of daily practice

Throughout the Day:

- **CAS Awareness Checks**: Set 3-4 random phone alerts. When they sound, notice: "What was my mind doing? Was I thinking about current activity or caught in worry/rumination?"
- **Attention Flexibility Practice**: When you notice mind-wandering during activities, practice returning attention to current task

Evening (5 minutes):

- **Daily Progress Review**: What did you notice about your attention patterns today? No analysis required—just observations

Week 1 Common Experiences:

Day 1-2: ATT feels awkward and artificial. Your mind wanders constantly during practice. You might forget to do evening reviews or miss attention checks.

This is completely normal. You're asking your brain to do something it's not used to doing. Like starting a new exercise routine, initial awkwardness is expected.

Day 3-4: You start noticing how often your mind is internally focused during daily activities. This awareness might initially feel uncomfortable—suddenly you're conscious of all the mental activity you previously ignored.

This increased awareness is progress, not a problem. You can't change mental patterns you don't recognize.

Day 5-7: ATT becomes slightly more familiar. You catch yourself in worry or rumination more quickly. You might have moments where attention focusing feels easier.

These small improvements matter. Every moment of increased attention flexibility is building neural pathways that support future change.

Week 1 Troubleshooting:

"I keep forgetting to practice":

- Link ATT to existing morning routine (before coffee, after shower)
- Set phone alarms for first week until habit establishes
- Lower expectations—even 3-4 practice sessions this week builds foundation

"My attention during ATT is terrible":

- Perfect attention isn't the goal—practice is the goal
- Mind-wandering during practice IS the practice (noticing and redirecting)
- Expect attention to be scattered initially

"I'm not noticing any changes":

- Week 1 changes are subtle and involve awareness rather than symptom relief
- Look for small shifts: slightly quicker recognition of mind-wandering, moments of easier attention focusing

- Benefits typically become more apparent in weeks 2-3

Week 2: Implementing worry postponement effectively

Week 2 introduces **worry postponement**—taking control of when you engage with worry concerns rather than letting worry dictate your mental schedule. This week you'll learn that timing matters more than content when it comes to managing worry.

Week 2 Primary Goals:

- Establish designated worry time
- Practice postponing non-urgent worries
- Distinguish between urgent concerns and worry cycles
- Continue building attention training consistency

Daily Practice Schedule:

Morning:

- **ATT Practice**: Continue 12-minute daily attention training
- **Worry Time Setup**: Set designated 15-20 minute worry period for early evening

Throughout the Day:

- **Worry Recognition**: Notice when worry thoughts arise
- **Immediate Action Test**: "Can I take useful action about this concern right now?"
    - If yes: Take appropriate action
    - If no: Use postponement response
- **Postponement Response**: "I'll think about this during worry time at [specific time]"

Evening:

- **Designated Worry Time**: Review postponed concerns
    - Notice how many concerns still feel urgent
    - Address concerns that require planning or problem-solving
    - Let go of concerns that have resolved naturally

Week 2 Progressive Practice:

Days 1-2: Start with relatively minor worries. Practice postponing concerns about schedule conflicts, minor social interactions, or work tasks that can't be immediately addressed.

Days 3-4: Apply postponement to moderate concerns. Try postponing worries about family members, work performance, or health issues that don't require immediate action.

Days 5-7: Practice with more emotionally charged worries. Test postponement with concerns that feel particularly urgent or important.

Week 2 Common Experiences:

Initial resistance: Your mind will insist that certain worries are too important to postpone. This feeling of urgency is often the worry itself, not the actual importance of the concern.

Surprise at natural resolution: Many people are shocked to discover how often postponed worries resolve themselves or lose emotional intensity by evening.

Inconsistent success: Some days postponement works easily; other days every worry feels too urgent to delay. This variation is normal and expected.

Improved daily focus: Even imperfect postponement often leads to better concentration during work and activities because mental energy isn't consumed by constant worry processing.

Week 3: Developing detached mindfulness skills

Week 3 introduces **detached mindfulness**—learning to observe thoughts as mental events rather than getting caught in their content. This week builds on the attention training foundation to develop a new relationship with your own thinking.

Week 3 Primary Goals:

- Learn to recognize thinking as mental activity rather than reality
- Practice stepping back from thought content
- Develop "no comment" responses to persistent thoughts
- Begin integrating detached mindfulness with worry postponement

Daily Practice Schedule:

Morning:

- **ATT Practice**: Continue 12-minute attention training
- **Detached Mindfulness Intention Setting**: "Today I'll practice observing thoughts as mental events"

Throughout the Day:

- **Thought Recognition Practice**: When you notice worry, rumination, or other CAS activity, practice: "I observe that my mind is producing [worry/rumination/analysis] thoughts about [brief topic]"
- **No Comment Practice**: For persistent or repetitive thoughts, practice responding with "No comment" and immediately redirecting attention
- **Detachment Experiments**: Practice seeing thoughts as passing mental events rather than problems to solve

Evening:

- **Worry Time with Detached Mindfulness**: During designated worry time, practice observing worry thoughts as mental content rather than absorbing into their emotional charge

Week 3 Progressive Skills:

Days 1-2: Focus on recognizing when you're thinking about thinking. Notice the difference between direct experience (eating lunch, talking to someone) and mental activity (analyzing experiences, predicting outcomes).

Days 3-4: Practice the basic detachment response: "I'm having the thought that..." before worry content. This simple phrase creates distance between you as observer and thoughts as mental events.

Days 5-7: Begin using "no comment" responses to persistent thoughts. Start with less emotionally charged thoughts before applying to major concerns.

Week 3 Skill Development Indicators:

Increased metacognitive awareness: You start noticing thinking activity more quickly after it begins rather than getting lost in thought content for extended periods.

Brief moments of detachment: Occasional experiences of observing thoughts without being pulled into their content, even if just for seconds.

Reduced thought urgency: Some thoughts begin feeling less immediately compelling or urgent, even if they still feel important.

Improved technique integration: Easier combination of attention training, worry postponement, and detached mindfulness during challenging moments.

Daily schedules and practice routines

Consistent daily practice is crucial for developing MCT skills. These schedules provide structure while allowing flexibility for individual lifestyles and constraints.

Standard Daily Schedule (Weeks 1-3):

Upon Waking (5 minutes):

- Set daily intention for MCT practice
- Brief body and mental state awareness
- Commit to practicing techniques as opportunities arise

Morning Practice (15 minutes):

- 12-minute Attention Training Technique
- 3-minute review of daily challenges where MCT techniques might be helpful

Midday Check-in (2 minutes):

- Quick assessment: "How has my attention been today? Have I been caught in any mental loops?"
- Reset intention for afternoon practice if needed

Evening Practice (20 minutes):

- 15-20 minute designated worry time (Week 2-3)
- 5-minute daily practice review: What worked? What was challenging?

Before Sleep (3 minutes):

- Brief detached mindfulness practice if rumination arises
- Set intention for tomorrow's practice

Modified Schedule for Busy Lifestyles:

Compressed Morning (8 minutes):

- 6-8 minute abbreviated ATT session
- Brief intention setting for day

Integrated Practice Throughout Day:

- Use transition times (commuting, waiting) for detached mindfulness practice
- Apply worry postponement during work breaks
- Practice attention redirection during routine activities

Evening (10 minutes):

- Combined worry time and practice review
- Quick planning for tomorrow's practice

Weekend Extended Practice:

- Full-length ATT sessions (12+ minutes)
- Extended detached mindfulness practice during leisure activities
- Weekly progress review and planning

Tracking sheets and progress indicators

Progress tracking during the foundation weeks focuses on process measures rather than outcome measures. You're building skills, not necessarily experiencing dramatic symptom relief yet.

Week 1 Tracking Sheet:

Daily ATT Practice:

Day 1: Completed? Y/N   Duration: ___ min   Attention wandering: Frequent/Moderate/Minimal

Day 2: Completed? Y/N   Duration: ___ min   Attention wandering: Frequent/Moderate/Minimal

Day 3: Completed? Y/N   Duration: ___ min   Attention wandering: Frequent/Moderate/Minimal

Day 4: Completed? Y/N   Duration: ___ min   Attention wandering: Frequent/Moderate/Minimal

Day 5: Completed? Y/N   Duration: ___ min   Attention wandering: Frequent/Moderate/Minimal

Day 6: Completed? Y/N   Duration: ___ min   Attention wandering: Frequent/Moderate/Minimal

Day 7: Completed? Y/N   Duration: ___ min   Attention wandering: Frequent/Moderate/Minimal

Daily CAS Awareness:

Day 1: Noticed worry/rumination episodes? Y/N   Estimated frequency: ___

Day 2: Noticed worry/rumination episodes? Y/N   Estimated frequency: ___

[Continue for all 7 days]

Week 1 Progress Indicators:

- Completing 5+ ATT sessions
- Increased awareness of mental activity patterns
- At least occasional success redirecting attention during daily activities
- Growing familiarity with MCT concepts and terminology

Week 2 Tracking Sheet:

Worry Postponement Practice:

Day 1: Worry time held? Y/N   Postponed worries: ___   Still urgent by evening: ___%

Day 2: Worry time held? Y/N   Postponed worries: ___   Still urgent by evening: ___%

[Continue for all 7 days]

Week 2 Progress Indicators:

- Successfully postponing at least 50% of non-urgent worries
- Noticing that many postponed concerns lose intensity by evening
- Improved concentration during daily activities
- Better distinction between urgent and non-urgent concerns

Week 3 Tracking Sheet:

Detached Mindfulness Practice:

Day 1: Practiced "no comment"? Y/N   Observed thoughts as events? Y/N   Integration success: 1-10

Day 2: Practiced "no comment"? Y/N   Observed thoughts as events? Y/N   Integration success: 1-10

[Continue for all 7 days]

Week 3 Progress Indicators:

- Occasional successful detachment from thought content
- Quicker recognition when caught in CAS patterns
- Brief moments of seeing thoughts as mental events rather than reality
- Beginning integration of multiple techniques simultaneously

Common week-by-week challenges and solutions

Each week of foundation building presents predictable challenges. Understanding these patterns helps normalize difficulties and provides specific solutions.

Week 1 Challenges:

Challenge: *"ATT feels boring and pointless"* Why this happens: Your brain is used to more stimulating mental activity. Attention training can initially feel understimulating. *Solution*: Remember ATT is like physical exercise—not always immediately enjoyable but beneficial over time. Focus on consistency rather than enjoyment.

Challenge: *"I can't tell if I'm doing anything right"* Why this happens: MCT improvements are often subtle and hard to detect initially. *Solution*: Focus on process goals (practicing daily, noticing when attention wanders) rather than outcome goals (feeling better immediately).

Challenge: *"My mind feels busier since starting MCT"* Why this happens: Increased awareness of mental activity that was always there but previously unconscious. *Solution*: This awareness is the first step of change, not a sign that things are getting worse.

Week 2 Challenges:

Challenge: *"Some worries feel too important to postpone"* Why this happens: Positive beliefs about worry make postponement feel irresponsible or risky. *Solution*: Start with clearly minor worries to build confidence, then gradually apply to more significant concerns.

Challenge: *"I keep forgetting about designated worry time"* Why this happens: If worry time isn't established as a routine, it's easy to skip when you're not actively worried. *Solution*: Set daily phone alarms and maintain worry time even when few concerns were postponed.

Challenge: *"Worry time becomes rumination time"* Why this happens: Without structure, designated worry time can become another opportunity for extended CAS activity. *Solution*: Set a timer, focus on actionable concerns, and stop when time is up regardless of "completion."

Week 3 Challenges:

Challenge: *"Detached mindfulness feels fake or forced"* Why this *happens*: You're learning a new way of relating to thoughts that initially feels unnatural. *Solution*: All new skills feel artificial initially. Focus on practicing the technique rather than having it feel natural immediately.

Challenge: *"I can't detach from really important thoughts"* Why this *happens*: Some thoughts carry emotional significance that makes detachment feel inappropriate or impossible. *Solution*: Practice detachment with minor thoughts first. Detachment doesn't mean thoughts aren't important—it means you can choose when to engage with them.

Challenge: *"Nothing feels like it's working together"* Why this *happens*: Learning multiple techniques simultaneously can feel overwhelming and disjointed. *Solution*: Each technique supports the others. Focus on one technique per week while maintaining others, rather than trying to master everything simultaneously.

Motivational checkpoints and celebration milestones

Foundation building requires motivation maintenance because benefits are often subtle and gradual. Regular checkpoints help you recognize progress and stay committed to practice.

Week 1 Celebration Milestones:

Day 3 Milestone: Completing three consecutive days of ATT practice *Celebration*: Acknowledge that you've begun rewiring your attention patterns—this is significant neuroplasticity

Day 5 Milestone: First successful recognition of CAS activity during daily life *Celebration*: You've developed metacognitive awareness—the foundation of all MCT techniques

Week 1 Completion: Practicing any form of attention training for seven consecutive days *Celebration*: You've established a new mental health routine and begun building attentional fitness

Week 2 Celebration Milestones:

First Successful Postponement: Successfully delaying any worry until designated time *Celebration*: You've broken the automatic worry response—you can choose when to engage with concerns

First Worry Resolution: Noticing that a postponed worry resolved naturally by evening *Celebration*: You've experienced evidence that many worries don't require immediate mental attention

Week 2 Completion: Maintaining both ATT and worry postponement practice *Celebration*: You're developing multiple MCT skills simultaneously and building a comprehensive practice

Week 3 Celebration Milestones:

First Thought Observation: Successfully observing a thought as a mental event rather than getting absorbed in its content *Celebration*: You've experienced the space between yourself and your thoughts—this is psychological freedom

First "No Comment" Success: Using the "no comment" technique to disengage from persistent thoughts *Celebration*: You've learned that not every thought requires a response—you can choose which thoughts deserve engagement

Three-Week Completion: Maintaining consistent practice across all foundation techniques *Celebration*: You've built the foundation for advanced MCT application and established sustainable practice routines

Creating Personal Celebration Rituals:

Small daily acknowledgments:

- Notice successful technique applications without over-analyzing them
- Give yourself brief positive recognition for practice consistency
- Share successes with supportive friends or family members

Weekly progress recognition:

- Review your tracking sheets to notice patterns of improvement
- Acknowledge efforts and consistency rather than only focusing on outcomes
- Plan small rewards for weekly practice completion (favorite activity, special meal, relaxation time)

Foundation completion recognition:

- After three weeks of practice, acknowledge that you've built genuine skills
- Notice specific examples of improved attention control or worry management
- Consider the cumulative effect of daily practice over 21 days

Building momentum for deeper change

The foundation weeks establish more than just familiarity with MCT techniques—they begin rewiring the automatic mental responses that maintain psychological problems. Research shows that consistent practice during these initial weeks predicts success in later stages of change (Hagen et al., 2017).

Neuroplasticity in Action:

Every time you redirect attention during ATT, you strengthen neural pathways associated with executive control. Every successful worry postponement builds confidence in your ability to choose when to engage with concerns. Every moment of detached mindfulness creates experience of the space between yourself and your thoughts.

These micro-changes accumulate into macro-changes that become apparent in weeks 4-6, when you'll challenge the deeper beliefs that maintain mental loops and integrate techniques into increasingly complex real-world situations.

Signs You're Ready for Deeper Work:

- You can complete ATT with occasional periods of sustained attention focus
- You successfully postpone at least 50% of non-urgent worries
- You've had at least brief experiences of observing thoughts as mental events
- You recognize CAS patterns more quickly when they begin
- You feel growing confidence in your ability to influence mental processes

If Foundation Building Feels Slow:

Remember that you're building skills that will serve you for years to come. Research consistently shows that people who establish strong foundation practices achieve better outcomes and maintain their gains longer than those who rush through basic skill development (Nordahl et al., 2018).

The patience you develop during foundation building is itself a valuable skill—learning to trust gradual process over immediate results, which is exactly the mental approach that supports psychological wellbeing.

Preparing for Advanced Practice:

These first three weeks establish the platform for more sophisticated MCT applications. You've learned to:

- Control attention flexibly rather than having it captured by internal concerns
- Choose when to engage with worry rather than responding automatically to every concern
- Observe thoughts as mental events rather than absorbing their content uncritically

These skills prepare you for the deeper work of weeks 4-6: challenging the metacognitive beliefs that maintain mental loops and integrating techniques into a seamless approach to mental health that works in all life situations.

Your foundation is solid. Now it's time to build on it.

Chapter 10: Weeks 4-6 - Deepening your practice

Rachel sits in her kitchen on Sunday morning, three weeks into her MCT practice, feeling simultaneously encouraged and frustrated. The techniques work—she can see that. Her worry postponement has shown her how many concerns resolve naturally. Her attention training has given her moments of genuine mental quiet. But she still feels pulled toward her old patterns, especially during stressful situations.

What if I never really change? she thinks, then catches herself. *Wait—there's my mind creating a "what if" scenario about my progress. And now I'm analyzing my analysis...* She laughs softly, realizing she's actually using detached mindfulness to observe her own worry about getting better.

This moment captures the essence of weeks 4-6: deeper self-awareness combined with more sophisticated skill application. You're no longer just learning techniques—you're developing a new way of being with your own mind.

Week 4: Challenging positive metacognitive beliefs

Week 4 marks a crucial transition from learning techniques to examining the beliefs that maintain mental loops. You've built foundation skills; now you'll challenge the assumptions that make worry and rumination feel necessary and beneficial.

Week 4 Primary Goals:

- Identify your strongest positive beliefs about worry and rumination
- Design behavioral experiments to test these beliefs

- Gather evidence about worry's actual effects on preparation and problem-solving
- Continue integrating foundation techniques while adding belief work

Understanding Your Positive Belief System:

Most people hold positive beliefs about worry and rumination without conscious awareness. These beliefs developed over time through cultural messages, family patterns, and personal experiences that seemed to confirm worry's value.

Common Positive Belief Categories:

Worry as Preparation:

- *"Worrying helps me be ready for problems"*
- *"If I think through all possibilities, I'll be prepared for anything"*
- *"Worry prevents me from being surprised by bad events"*

Worry as Care:

- *"Worrying about my family shows I love them"*
- *"If I don't worry about important things, I'm being careless"*
- *"Good parents/partners/employees worry about their responsibilities"*

Rumination as Understanding:

- *"I need to analyze my problems to understand them"*
- *"Thinking deeply about my mistakes helps me learn from them"*
- *"If I don't figure out why something happened, it might happen again"*

Week 4 Daily Practice Schedule:

Morning:

- **ATT Practice**: Continue 12-minute attention training
- **Belief Identification**: Each morning, notice one positive belief about worry or rumination that feels particularly true

Throughout the Day:

- **Belief Testing Setup**: When you notice worry or rumination beginning, pause and ask: "What do I believe this mental activity will accomplish?"
- **Evidence Collection**: Notice actual outcomes of worry episodes vs. predicted benefits
- **Continue Postponement**: Maintain worry time while observing beliefs about why postponement feels difficult

Evening:

- **Worry Time + Belief Analysis**: During designated worry time, notice what beliefs drive your engagement with specific concerns
- **Evidence Review**: What evidence did you collect today about worry's actual effects vs. predicted benefits?

Week 4 Behavioral Experiments:

Experiment 1: The Preparation Test

Target belief: "Worry helps me prepare for important events"

Design:

- Choose two similar upcoming situations (meetings, social events, challenging conversations)
- **Situation A**: Worry extensively beforehand as you normally would

- **Situation B**: Do minimal worry, focus on concrete preparation actions only

Evidence to collect:

- Which situation felt more prepared for in advance?
- Which situation actually went better?
- Which approach led to better problem-solving when unexpected issues arose?
- How did you feel during each situation?

Common findings: Most people discover that worry feels like preparation but doesn't actually improve readiness. Concrete action-oriented preparation proves more effective than mental rehearsal of problems.

Experiment 2: The Problem-Solving Test

Target belief: "Ruminating about my problems helps me find solutions"

Design:

- Choose a current life problem you've been thinking about extensively
- **Week A**: Allow unlimited rumination about this problem, tracking insights and solutions generated
- **Week B**: Limit problem consideration to 15 minutes of action-oriented problem-solving twice weekly

Evidence to collect:

- How many practical solutions emerged from each approach?
- Which approach led to actual problem-solving action?
- How did each approach affect your mood and energy?

- Which approach provided genuine insights vs. repetitive analysis?

Experiment 3: The Care Test

Target belief: "I need to worry about my family to show I care about them"

Design:

- **Week A**: Express care primarily through worry and mental concern about family members
- **Week B**: Express care through attention, presence, and helpful action while postponing worry about them

Evidence to collect:

- Which approach felt more caring to you?
- How did family members respond to each approach?
- Which approach actually contributed more to family wellbeing?
- Which approach left you with more energy for family relationships?

Week 5: Addressing negative beliefs about control

Week 5 targets the beliefs that make mental loops feel inescapable and dangerous. These **negative metacognitive beliefs** create fear around thinking itself and maintain the urgency that keeps CAS patterns active.

Week 5 Primary Goals:

- Identify and examine negative beliefs about thought control
- Test beliefs about the dangers of worry and rumination
- Gather evidence about your actual level of mental control

- Experience that thoughts are not dangerous, even when uncomfortable

Common Negative Belief Categories:

Uncontrollability Beliefs:
- *"I have no control over my worrying"*
- *"Once I start ruminating, I can't stop"*
- *"My thoughts have a mind of their own"*
- *"I'm helpless against my anxiety"*

Danger Beliefs:
- *"Worrying too much could make me lose my mind"*
- *"If I can't control these thoughts, something's seriously wrong with me"*
- *"These feelings might overwhelm me completely"*
- *"My anxiety could cause me to have a breakdown"*

Meaning Beliefs:
- *"Having these thoughts means I'm not normal"*
- *"These thoughts reveal something terrible about my character"*
- *"If I'm thinking this, it must be important"*
- *"Normal people don't have thoughts like this"*

Week 5 Daily Practice Schedule:

Morning:
- **ATT Practice**: Continue attention training while noticing beliefs about your ability to control attention

- **Control Belief Check**: Notice thoughts about whether you "should" be able to control your mental state better

Throughout the Day:

- **Control Evidence Collection**: Notice examples of mental control you actually do have (choosing to focus on tasks, redirecting attention, decision-making)
- **Danger Belief Testing**: When worry or rumination feels dangerous or overwhelming, experiment with allowing it to continue briefly while observing what actually happens

Evening:

- **Worry Time + Control Assessment**: During worry time, notice that you can choose when to start and stop worry engagement
- **Daily Control Evidence Review**: What examples of actual mental control did you observe today?

Week 5 Behavioral Experiments:

Experiment 1: The Control Test

Target belief: "I have no control over my worry"

Design:

- Choose a moderate-level worry topic
- **Day 1**: Try to worry about this topic for exactly 10 minutes, then stop
- **Day 2**: Try to avoid worrying about this topic entirely for 2 hours
- **Day 3**: Postpone worry about this topic until evening, then engage for 15 minutes

- **Day 4**: Use detached mindfulness when worry about this topic arises

Evidence to collect:

- How much control did you actually have in each condition?
- What techniques gave you the most sense of control?
- Was control completely absent, or partial but real?
- How does this evidence compare to your belief about having "no control"?

Experiment 2: The Danger Test

Target belief: "Worrying too much could make me lose control"

Design:

- During a designated 15-minute period, try to worry as intensively as possible about your most concerning topic
- Allow the worry to be as dramatic and catastrophic as your mind wants to make it
- Observe what actually happens to your mental state, behavior, and sense of control

Evidence to collect:

- Did intensive worry lead to loss of control or "going crazy"?
- What were the actual effects of deliberately intense worry?
- How quickly did you return to normal mental functioning afterward?
- Was the experience dangerous, or just unpleasant?

Safety note: Use moderate worry topics for this experiment, not traumatic or severely distressing concerns.

Experiment 3: The Meaning Test

Target belief: "Having unwanted thoughts means something significant about me"

Design:

- For one week, track all random, bizarre, or unwanted thoughts that arise
- Notice thoughts that don't reflect your values, desires, or intentions
- Observe the difference between having thoughts and acting on thoughts

Evidence to collect:

- How many random thoughts do you have that don't reflect your actual character?
- What's the relationship between unwanted thoughts and your actual behavior?
- Do other people seem to be defined by their random thoughts, or by their actions?
- What evidence suggests that thoughts reveal "true" personality vs. normal brain activity?

Week 6: Integrating all techniques seamlessly

Week 6 focuses on smooth integration of all MCT techniques into a coherent approach. Instead of using techniques separately, you'll learn to combine them fluidly as situations require.

Week 6 Primary Goals:

- Combine attention training, worry postponement, and detached mindfulness seamlessly
- Apply integrated MCT response to challenging real-world situations

- Develop automatic recognition and response to CAS activation
- Build confidence in comprehensive MCT application

Week 6 Integrated Daily Practice:

Morning Integrated Practice (20 minutes):

- **ATT with Belief Awareness**: During attention training, notice any beliefs about your performance or progress, and practice detached mindfulness with these beliefs
- **Daily Challenge Preparation**: Identify likely challenging situations today and mentally rehearse integrated MCT responses

Real-Time Integration Throughout Day:

- **The Three-Step Integration Response**:
    1. **Recognize**: Notice CAS activation (worry, rumination, threat monitoring)
    2. **Choose**: Select appropriate technique(s) based on situation
    3. **Apply**: Implement technique while maintaining awareness of metacognitive beliefs

Evening Integration Practice:

- **Comprehensive Worry Time**: Use designated worry time to practice belief challenging, evidence review, and technique integration
- **Daily Integration Review**: How successfully did you combine techniques today?

Week 6 Advanced Scenarios:

Scenario 1: Work Presentation Anxiety *Integrated MCT Response*:

- **ATT skills**: Focus attention on presentation preparation rather than anxiety management
- **Worry postponement**: Postpone concerns about audience reactions until after presentation
- **Detached mindfulness**: Observe pre-presentation anxiety thoughts without engaging their content
- **Belief challenging**: Test belief that worry improves performance by comparing worried vs. non-worried preparation effectiveness

Scenario 2: Relationship Conflict *Integrated MCT Response*:

- **ATT skills**: Maintain attention on current conversation rather than mental rehearsal of arguments
- **Worry postponement**: Postpone concerns about relationship implications until private reflection time
- **Detached mindfulness**: Observe mind-reading attempts and self-critical thoughts without engaging
- **Belief challenging**: Test beliefs about whether worry protects relationships vs. interferes with connection

Scenario 3: Health Concerns *Integrated MCT Response*:

- **ATT skills**: Focus attention on appropriate medical care rather than symptom monitoring
- **Worry postponement**: Postpone health catastrophizing until designated worry time
- **Detached mindfulness**: Observe health anxiety thoughts without engaging their content
- **Belief challenging**: Test beliefs about whether health worry prevents illness vs. creates unnecessary distress

Advanced exercises and experiments

Week 4-6 includes more sophisticated applications of MCT principles designed to challenge deeper assumptions and create more robust skill application.

Advanced Attention Training Variations:

Environmental ATT: Practice attention training in challenging environments (busy cafes, noisy locations) to build real-world attention flexibility.

Emotional ATT: Practice attention training when experiencing mild anxiety or frustration to develop attention control during emotional activation.

Distraction-Enhanced ATT: Practice attention training while deliberately exposed to mild distractions (background conversations, visual movement) to strengthen attention control under challenging conditions.

Advanced Belief Challenging Experiments:

The "Worry as Much as Possible" Experiment:

Target: Any positive belief about worry's benefits

Design:

- Choose one current concern
- **Day 1**: Worry about this concern as much as possible throughout the day
- **Day 2**: Use worry postponement and detached mindfulness for the same concern
- **Day 3**: Use problem-solving approach (15 minutes of action-oriented thinking) for the same concern

Advanced evidence collection:

- Which approach led to the most creative solutions?

- Which approach preserved the most mental energy for other activities?

- Which approach felt most caring if the concern involved other people?

- Which approach led to the most effective action?

The "Loss of Control" Experiment:

Target: Beliefs about the dangers of intense emotion or worry

Design:

- In a safe environment, deliberately induce mild anxiety or worry about a manageable concern

- Allow the feeling to be as intense as it naturally becomes without trying to control it

- Observe what actually happens to your thinking, behavior, and functioning

- Notice your capacity to function normally even with uncomfortable internal experiences

Evidence focus:

- Did allowing intense feeling lead to loss of control?

- How long did intense emotion naturally last when not fought?

- What evidence do you have about your ability to handle uncomfortable internal experiences?

Handling setbacks and resistance

Weeks 4-6 often include periods of resistance or apparent setbacks as you challenge deeper assumptions. Understanding these patterns helps you navigate challenges without abandoning practice.

Common Week 4-6 Resistance Patterns:

Intellectual Resistance: *"This belief challenging stuff is just mental games. My worries are real problems."*

Understanding the resistance: Your positive beliefs about worry are being threatened, which can feel like your coping system is under attack.

Working with resistance: Use the resistance as data. Notice: "I'm having thoughts that belief challenging is pointless. These thoughts might be protecting my current worry patterns."

Moving forward: Approach belief challenging as experimental rather than threatening. You're collecting data, not attacking your coping system.

Emotional Resistance: *"It feels wrong to stop worrying about people I care about."*

Understanding the resistance: Challenging positive beliefs can feel like becoming less caring or responsible.

Working with resistance: Distinguish between care and worry. Experiment with expressing care through attention, presence, and action rather than mental concern.

Moving forward: Test whether worry actually helps the people you care about, or whether presence and action are more beneficial.

Practical Resistance: *"These techniques work in practice sessions but not in real-life stress."*

Understanding the resistance: Real-world application always feels more challenging than controlled practice.

Working with resistance: Expect imperfect application during stress. Focus on partial success rather than perfect technique implementation.

Moving forward: Start with lower-stress situations and gradually apply techniques to more challenging circumstances.

Setback Recovery Strategies:

The "Setback as Information" Approach: When you experience setbacks, use them as learning opportunities:

- What specific situation triggered return to old patterns?
- Which techniques were most difficult to access during stress?
- What beliefs became strongest during challenging moments?
- How can you modify your approach based on this information?

The "Partial Success Recognition" Method: Instead of all-or-nothing thinking about progress:

- Notice any moments of increased awareness during difficult periods
- Acknowledge quicker recovery from mental loops, even if they still occur
- Recognize that using techniques imperfectly is still progress over not using them at all

Fine-tuning your personal approach

By week 6, you'll have enough experience to customize MCT techniques to your specific patterns, challenges, and lifestyle. This personalization makes techniques more sustainable and effective.

Personalizing Attention Training:

For visual learners: Experiment with visual attention training using environmental details rather than only auditory stimuli

For busy schedules: Develop abbreviated ATT versions (6-8 minutes) that can be used consistently rather than skipping practice entirely

For high-stress environments: Practice attention training in gradually more challenging environments to build real-world application skills

Customizing Worry Postponement:

For morning worriers: Create morning worry time in addition to or instead of evening sessions

For work-related anxiety: Develop separate work worry time to handle professional concerns distinctly from personal worries

For parents: Modify postponement to distinguish between appropriate parental concern and unnecessary worry cycles

Adapting Detached Mindfulness:

For analytical thinkers: Use scientific metaphors (thoughts as data rather than commands) to make detachment feel more natural

For emotional processors: Develop detachment approaches that honor emotional experience while reducing engagement with worry content

For people-pleasers: Practice detaching from thoughts about others' opinions while maintaining attention to actual relationship needs

Personal MCT Signature:

By week 6, develop your personal MCT approach:

Primary technique: Which single MCT technique feels most natural and effective for you?

Backup technique: Which technique works best when your primary approach isn't accessible?

Challenging situation technique: Which approach works best during your most difficult mental loop triggers?

Daily maintenance approach: What combination of techniques can you maintain long-term without burden?

Case studies of successful progression

Understanding how others navigate weeks 4-6 provides models for working through your own challenges and resistance.

Case Study 1: Jennifer - The Perfectionist

Background: Marketing executive with performance anxiety and worry about making mistakes

Week 4 Focus: Challenging belief that "I need to worry about details to prevent mistakes"

Experiment: Compared preparing for client presentations with extensive worry vs. concrete preparation without worry focus *Results*: "I was amazed that I actually made fewer mistakes when I wasn't constantly worried about making them. My brain had more space for actual thinking."

Week 5 Focus: Addressing belief that "If I make mistakes, people will think I'm incompetent"

Experiment: Deliberately made small, recoverable mistakes in low-stakes situations and observed actual reactions *Results*: "Most people barely noticed my minor mistakes, and when they did, they were understanding rather than judgmental."

Week 6 Integration: Combined attention training during meetings, worry postponement about performance outcomes, and detached mindfulness with self-critical thoughts

Outcome: "I started enjoying my work again. I had no idea how much mental energy worry was consuming until I learned to redirect it."

Case Study 2: Michael - The Health Worrier

Background: 45-year-old teacher with health anxiety following minor cardiac episode

Week 4 Focus: Challenging belief that "I need to monitor my body constantly to stay healthy"

Experiment: Compared days of intensive body monitoring vs. normal health awareness without hypervigilance *Results*: "Constant monitoring made me feel sicker, not safer. I was finding problems that weren't there."

Week 5 Focus: Addressing belief that "Having health anxiety means something is seriously wrong"

Experiment: Researched prevalence of health anxiety and talked with others about their health concerns *Results*: "I learned that health anxiety is incredibly common and doesn't indicate actual illness. It's just how some minds respond to body awareness."

Week 6 Integration: Used attention training during medical appointments, worry postponement for health concerns that couldn't be immediately addressed, and detached mindfulness with catastrophic health thoughts

Outcome: "I can now go to doctor appointments without spending the week before imagining worst-case scenarios. I take care of my health without being terrorized by my body."

Case Study 3: Lisa - The Relationship Ruminator

Background: Graduate student with social anxiety and tendency to replay social interactions

Week 4 Focus: Challenging belief that "I need to analyze social interactions to improve my relationships"

Experiment: Compared weeks of extensive social analysis vs. weeks focused on present-moment social engagement *Results*: "My relationships actually improved when I stopped analyzing them constantly. I was more present and responsive to people."

Week 5 Focus: Addressing belief that "My social anxiety thoughts reveal what others really think of me"

Experiment: Tested social predictions against reality by asking trusted friends about their actual perceptions *Results*: "My anxious thoughts were terrible predictors of what people actually thought. They reflected my anxiety, not reality."

Week 6 Integration: Combined all techniques into social situations—attention training for present-moment focus, postponement for social analysis, detached mindfulness with self-critical thoughts

Outcome: "Social interactions became enjoyable again. I could focus on connecting with people rather than managing my anxiety about connecting with people."

Consolidating your transformation

Weeks 4-6 represent the heart of MCT transformation—the period where technique practice becomes genuine skill and surface-level change develops into deeper shifts in how you relate to your own mind.

Signs of Deep Change:

Automatic technique access: MCT responses begin happening spontaneously rather than requiring conscious effort to remember and apply

Reduced belief conviction: Old assumptions about worry and rumination feel less obviously true and more like opinions that can be questioned

Increased mental flexibility: You notice more options for responding to thoughts and emotions rather than feeling compelled toward automatic reactions

Improved reality testing: Better discrimination between mental content (thoughts, predictions, interpretations) and actual current circumstances

Enhanced emotional resilience: Difficult emotions feel more manageable because you're not adding mental loops on top of natural emotional responses

These weeks prepare you for the maintenance phase, where MCT becomes not something you do but part of how you naturally relate to your own mental experience. The foundation you built in weeks 1-3 and the deep work of weeks 4-6 create lasting change that can withstand life's inevitable challenges and stresses.

You're not just learning to manage symptoms—you're developing a fundamentally different relationship with your own mind that supports wellbeing regardless of external circumstances.

Chapter 11: Week 7 and beyond - Maintaining your gains

Maria sits in her car outside the grocery store, phone buzzing with a text from her boss about a "quick chat" tomorrow morning. Six months ago, this would have triggered a three-hour mental spiral about potential job problems, performance reviews, and financial catastrophe. Today, something different happens.

She notices the familiar worry thought beginning (*What does he want to discuss?*), observes it as a mental event rather than an emergency broadcast, and thinks: *I'll find out tomorrow what he wants to discuss. Right now, I'm going grocery shopping.* She puts her phone away and walks into the store, present and calm.

This moment illustrates what successful MCT integration looks like—not the absence of all worry thoughts, but a fundamentally different relationship with them. The techniques have become less like tools you consciously apply and more like natural responses that happen automatically.

Consolidating your new mental habits

After six weeks of structured practice, you've built new neural pathways and established different default responses to mental challenges. Week 7 focuses on strengthening these new patterns and ensuring they become your automatic responses rather than effortful techniques.

The Habit Consolidation Process:

Research in neuroplasticity shows that new mental habits become truly automatic through three stages:

Stage 1 (Weeks 1-3): Conscious practice of new responses while old patterns remain stronger **Stage 2 (Weeks 4-6)**: New patterns gain strength while old patterns weaken **Stage 3 (Week 7+)**: New patterns become default responses with minimal conscious effort

Week 7 Consolidation Goals:

Automatic Recognition: CAS activation becomes immediately obvious rather than requiring conscious monitoring

Effortless Response: MCT techniques feel natural rather than forced or artificial

Flexible Application: Smooth adaptation of techniques to new situations without rigid adherence to original practice formats

Confident Implementation: Trust in your ability to handle mental challenges as they arise

Week 7 Practice Evolution:

Modified ATT Practice:

- Reduce formal ATT to 4-5 times weekly rather than daily
- Use attention training principles during challenging real-world situations
- Practice attention switching during conversations, meetings, and daily activities
- Apply selective attention skills when focused work is required

Integrated Worry Management:

- Worry postponement becomes automatic response to non-urgent concerns
- Designated worry time becomes action-oriented problem-solving rather than repetitive concern

- Natural discrimination between actionable concerns and mental noise

Seamless Detached Mindfulness:

- Observation of thoughts as mental events becomes default mode rather than conscious technique
- "No comment" responses happen automatically with persistent rumination
- Detachment from thought content while maintaining engagement with life activities

Creating your long-term maintenance plan

Successful MCT maintenance requires a sustainable approach that fits your lifestyle and continues building skills without becoming burdensome.

Maintenance Practice Structure:

Daily Minimums (10-15 minutes total):

- **Morning intention setting** (2 minutes): Brief awareness of mental state and commitment to MCT principles for the day
- **Midday check-in** (1 minute): Quick assessment of attention focus and CAS activity
- **Evening review** (2-3 minutes): Notice successful technique applications and challenges faced

Weekly Intensive Practice (30-45 minutes):

- **Extended ATT session** (15-20 minutes): Longer attention training to maintain attentional flexibility
- **Belief review and challenging** (15 minutes): Examine any metacognitive beliefs that became problematic during the week

- **Technique refinement** (10-15 minutes): Practice MCT applications for anticipated challenging situations

Monthly Assessment and Adjustment (60 minutes):

- **Progress evaluation**: Compare current mental patterns to pre-MCT patterns
- **Technique effectiveness review**: Which approaches work best for your current life circumstances?
- **Challenge identification**: What new situations or stressors require adapted MCT application?
- **Practice modification**: Adjust maintenance routines based on what you've learned about your patterns and needs

Maintenance Practice Options:

Minimalist Approach (for busy lifestyles):

- 5 minutes morning ATT practice
- Automatic worry postponement and detached mindfulness throughout day
- Brief weekly technique review

Standard Approach (balanced maintenance):

- 10-15 minutes daily structured practice
- Weekly technique refinement sessions
- Monthly progress assessment and planning

Enhanced Approach (for complex challenges or high stress periods):

- Daily ATT and belief work
- Regular behavioral experiments with new challenges
- Integration of MCT principles into major life decisions and relationships

Recognizing and preventing relapse

MCT research shows lower relapse rates compared to traditional therapies, but understanding relapse warning signs and prevention strategies ensures long-term success (Solem et al., 2019).

Early Warning Signs of Potential Relapse:

Gradual Technique Abandonment:

- Skipping daily practice "just for today" repeatedly
- Returning to old problem-solving approaches during stress
- Forgetting to apply MCT techniques during challenging situations
- Resuming extended worry and rumination without postponement

Belief System Reversion:

- Old positive beliefs about worry feeling true again
- Negative beliefs about control returning during stressful periods
- Abandoning experimental approaches to metacognitive beliefs
- Returning to analysis and mental control efforts

Attention Pattern Regression:

- Increased internal focus and decreased environmental awareness
- Difficulty maintaining attention on current activities
- Return of hypervigilance and threat monitoring
- Loss of attention flexibility during daily tasks

CAS Pattern Reactivation:

- Extended worry episodes returning to previous frequency
- Rumination lasting longer and feeling more compelling
- Increased avoidance and safety-seeking behaviors
- Return of urgent feelings about mental control

Relapse Prevention Strategies:

Early Intervention Protocol: When you notice warning signs, immediately:

1. **Increase practice frequency** temporarily (return to daily ATT and structured worry time)
2. **Re-examine beliefs** that may have reverted to old patterns
3. **Simplify technique application** rather than abandoning techniques entirely
4. **Seek support** from MCT-trained professionals or supportive others familiar with your MCT practice

Stress Period Modifications: During high-stress life periods (job changes, relationship challenges, health issues):

- **Increase maintenance practice** temporarily without self-criticism
- **Lower performance expectations** for technique application
- **Focus on core techniques** (ATT and worry postponement) rather than trying to maintain all skills perfectly
- **Use MCT principles** to guide decision-making during stressful periods

Proactive Relapse Prevention:

Quarterly Practice Reviews: Every three months, assess your MCT practice and make adjustments before problems develop

Stress Period Planning: Before entering predictably stressful periods, plan how you'll maintain MCT practice and what modifications might be necessary

Support System Development: Build relationships with others who understand MCT principles or can support your practice during challenging times

Continued Learning: Stay engaged with MCT concepts through reading, workshops, or additional training to keep skills fresh and evolving

Adapting techniques for life changes

Life inevitably brings changes that require adapting your MCT practice. Career transitions, relationship changes, health challenges, family developments, and aging all present new contexts for applying MCT principles.

Career Transition Applications:

Job searching stress: Use MCT techniques to handle uncertainty about employment outcomes, rejection anxiety, and performance pressure during interviews

New role adjustment: Apply attention training to learning new skills rather than worrying about competence; use worry postponement for concerns about fitting in or meeting expectations

Retirement transition: Adapt techniques to handle identity changes and increased unstructured time that might allow more rumination

Relationship Change Applications:

New relationship development: Use detached mindfulness with relationship anxiety and future outcome worries; apply attention training to present-moment relationship building

Marriage and partnership: Integrate MCT approaches into conflict resolution and shared decision-making; use techniques to handle normal relationship uncertainty

Parenting stages: Adapt worry postponement for child-related concerns; use detached mindfulness with parenting guilt and comparative worry about child development

Divorce or relationship ending: Apply MCT principles to processing loss without getting stuck in rumination; use techniques to handle single life uncertainty

Health Challenge Applications:

Acute illness: Use detached mindfulness with health catastrophizing; apply worry postponement to medical outcome concerns beyond your control

Chronic conditions: Integrate MCT with medical care to handle uncertainty and lifestyle changes without adding unnecessary mental suffering

Aging concerns: Apply techniques to worry about cognitive changes, physical limitations, and mortality without eliminating appropriate health awareness

Family Change Applications:

Children leaving home: Use MCT to handle "empty nest" transitions and worry about adult children's independence

Aging parents: Apply techniques to appropriate concern vs. excessive worry about parents' health and wellbeing

Family crises: Use MCT principles during genuine family emergencies to maintain clear thinking and effective action

Building resilience for future challenges

Long-term MCT practice builds what researchers call **metacognitive resilience**—the ability to handle mental challenges that haven't been specifically practiced or anticipated.

Components of Metacognitive Resilience:

Flexible Attention: Ability to direct attention intentionally regardless of environmental stressors or emotional states

Belief Flexibility: Comfort questioning and testing mental assumptions rather than automatically accepting them as true

Uncertainty Tolerance: Capacity to function effectively without needing to resolve all questions or control all outcomes

Mental Process Awareness: Ongoing recognition of thinking patterns and metacognitive beliefs as they operate

Response Choice: Automatic access to multiple options for responding to thoughts and emotions rather than single default reactions

Building Resilience Through Advanced Practice:

Scenario Planning: Mentally rehearse how you'd apply MCT principles to challenges you haven't yet faced (job loss, health crises, relationship problems, family emergencies)

Cross-Training: Practice applying MCT techniques to positive emotions and experiences, not just negative ones (excitement, anticipation, creative thoughts)

Teaching Others: Explain MCT concepts to family members or friends, which deepens your own understanding and provides practice articulating principles clearly

Continued Challenge: Regularly apply MCT techniques to new, moderately stressful situations to prevent skills from becoming rigid or limited to familiar contexts

Graduate-level MCT practices

After establishing solid foundation and maintenance practices, some people choose to develop more advanced MCT applications that deepen understanding and expand capabilities.

Advanced Metacognitive Awareness:

Thought Process Discrimination: Learning to distinguish between different types of thinking (creative, analytical, worry, rumination, planning) and responding appropriately to each

Belief System Mapping: Developing comprehensive awareness of your personal metacognitive belief system and how different beliefs interact

Emotional Metacognition: Applying MCT principles to beliefs about emotions ("Anger is dangerous," "Sadness means I'm weak") rather than only beliefs about thoughts

Advanced Attention Applications:

Attention in Relationships: Using attention training principles to enhance listening skills, emotional presence, and conflict resolution

Professional Attention: Applying attention flexibility to complex work tasks, leadership challenges, and professional development

Creative Attention: Using attention training to support artistic, innovative, or problem-solving activities

Advanced Integration Applications:

Life Philosophy Integration: Incorporating MCT principles into major life decisions, value clarification, and goal-setting processes

Spiritual or Existential Applications: Using MCT approaches with questions about meaning, purpose, mortality, and life direction

Advanced Helping Skills: Learning to support others using MCT principles without becoming their therapist

Community and support resources

Long-term MCT practice benefits from connection with others who understand these principles and can provide support during challenging periods.

Professional Resources:

MCT-Trained Therapists: For complex issues or additional support, work with professionals specifically trained in MCT through the MCT Institute

MCT Training Programs: Consider attending workshops or training programs to deepen your understanding and connect with others practicing MCT

Professional Consultation: Periodic check-ins with MCT professionals can help refine technique application and troubleshoot persistent challenges

Community Resources:

MCT Practice Groups: Some communities have support groups for people practicing MCT principles

Online Communities: Forums and social media groups focused on metacognitive approaches to mental health

Educational Resources: Books, articles, and videos that continue expanding your MCT knowledge and application skills

Personal Support Network:

MCT-Informed Friends and Family: Share MCT principles with close others so they can support your practice and potentially benefit themselves

Accountability Partners: Work with friends or family members who are also interested in improving their mental habits

Professional Networks: Workplace colleagues or professional associations interested in stress management and performance enhancement

Your ongoing journey

MCT isn't a destination you reach but a way of traveling through life. The techniques you've learned provide a foundation for handling whatever mental challenges arise, but the real value lies in the changed relationship with your own mind.

Long-term MCT Practice Means:

You notice mental loops quickly and have multiple options for responding rather than getting trapped automatically

You trust your ability to handle psychological challenges without needing to control every thought or emotion

You engage with life from present-moment awareness rather than constant mental time travel to past regrets or future fears

You make decisions based on your values and goals rather than being driven by anxiety, worry, or rumination

You maintain perspective during difficult periods because you understand that thoughts and emotions are temporary mental events rather than permanent reality

You help others by modeling a healthy relationship with mental challenges and sharing what you've learned when appropriate

The most successful MCT practitioners describe it not as a set of techniques they use, but as a way of being that supports wellbeing, effectiveness, and genuine enjoyment of life. You've learned not just how to manage mental loops, but how to live with psychological freedom.

Your practice continues to deepen and expand, supporting not just symptom relief but genuine flourishing—the ability to engage fully with life's challenges and opportunities from a place of mental clarity and emotional resilience.

The invitation remains open: to continue growing in your ability to live with awareness, choice, and freedom in relationship to your own mind.

Part IV: Special Applications and Advanced Strategies

Chapter 12: MCT for Specific Anxiety Patterns

Different types of anxiety create their own unique mental loops, but the beautiful thing about MCT is that the same core principles work across all patterns. Once you understand how metacognition drives your specific anxiety, you can customize the techniques to break free from whatever trap has been holding you back.

Think of anxiety disorders as different flavors of the same underlying problem. Social anxiety makes you hyper-focused on yourself, health anxiety turns your body into a threat detector, panic disorder creates fear of your own fear, OCD gets you stuck in endless checking loops, and PTSD keeps replaying past trauma. Different symptoms, same metacognitive engine underneath.

The research consistently shows that **MCT works across anxiety disorders with success rates between 70-85%** (Wells, 2009). What changes isn't the approach but how you apply the techniques to your particular pattern of worry and rumination.

Social Anxiety and Self-Focused Attention

Social anxiety creates what researchers call *self-focused attention* – your mental spotlight turns inward at exactly the wrong moment. When you need to connect with others, your brain becomes obsessed with monitoring yourself instead. You're analyzing your performance, checking for signs of embarrassment, and predicting social disasters while the actual conversation happens around you.

Sarah's story illustrates this perfectly. She'd walk into meetings already rehearsing what she might say, then spend the entire time monitoring whether people looked bored by her contributions. After meetings, she'd replay every interaction, analyzing facial expressions and tone of voice for signs of rejection. The more she monitored herself, the more awkward and disconnected she became.

The MCT approach targets this self-monitoring directly. Instead of trying to think more positive thoughts or challenging social predictions, you learn to redirect attention away from self-monitoring altogether.

Attention refocusing for social situations: Start with external attention anchoring. Before social interactions, spend 30 seconds focusing completely on your environment – the sounds, colors, textures around you. This primes your brain for outward attention rather than inward monitoring.

During conversations, use what we call *conversational anchoring*. Pick one specific thing about the other person to focus on – their voice tone, the way they gesture, or the content of what they're saying. When you notice self-monitoring starting, gently redirect to your chosen anchor.

Modified worry postponement: Social anxiety often involves pre-event worry ("What if I say something stupid?") and post-event analysis ("Did I offend them?"). Apply postponement to both ends. Before social events, tell pre-worries: "I'll think about this afterward if it's still important." After events, tell post-analysis thoughts: "I'll review this tomorrow during worry time if it matters."

Research shows that **87% of social predictions never happen** (Clark & Wells, 1995), and **73% of post-event analysis concerns prove unfounded** when examined 24 hours later. Your worry postponement practice will demonstrate this reality.

Detached mindfulness for social thoughts: When thoughts like "They think I'm boring" or "I'm making no sense" arise, treat them as mental events rather than facts requiring investigation. Use the *social thoughts are just noise* approach – acknowledge them like background music while keeping your attention on the actual interaction.

Health Anxiety and Body Monitoring

Health anxiety turns your body into a full-time surveillance project. Every sensation becomes potential evidence of serious illness, creating what researchers call *somatic hypervigilance* – an exhausting state of constant body monitoring that actually creates more symptoms to worry about.

Michael spent hours each day checking his pulse, examining skin changes, and researching symptoms online. The more he monitored, the more irregularities he found. His attention had become a symptom-finding machine, interpreting normal bodily variations as medical emergencies.

The metacognitive trap in health anxiety involves two key beliefs:

1. "If I monitor carefully enough, I can prevent serious illness"
2. "Ignoring symptoms would be dangerous and irresponsible"

Both beliefs keep you trapped in monitoring cycles that increase anxiety rather than providing actual health security.

Breaking the monitoring cycle: Apply attention training specifically to body awareness. Instead of trying to ignore physical sensations, practice directing attention to external stimuli while acknowledging that body sensations exist in the background. This isn't denial – it's appropriate attention allocation.

Create *monitoring postponement periods*. When the urge to check symptoms arises, postpone for increasingly longer intervals. Start with 15 minutes, then 30 minutes, then hours. Most symptom concerns resolve naturally when not fed with constant attention.

The body scan paradox: Traditional mindfulness often recommends body scanning, but for health anxiety, this can worsen monitoring habits. Instead, use *selective attention body check-ins* – brief, scheduled moments of body awareness (morning and evening) rather than continuous monitoring throughout the day.

Research demonstrates that **excessive body monitoring increases symptom reporting by 340%** while actual health outcomes remain unchanged (Barsky & Ahern, 2004). Your attention training will reverse this pattern, allowing normal body awareness without pathological monitoring.

Panic Attacks and Fear of Fear

Panic disorder creates a unique metacognitive trap: you become afraid of your own fear response. This *fear of fear* pattern maintains panic through anticipatory anxiety and safety behaviors that actually increase vulnerability to panic attacks.

The metacognitive model explains panic through three levels:

1. **Initial trigger** (could be anything – physical sensation, thought, situation)
2. **Catastrophic interpretation** ("I'm having a heart attack")
3. **Meta-worry about panic** ("What if I panic again?")

Jessica's panic started with occasional work stress but evolved into constant fear of panic itself. She'd monitor her heart rate, avoid triggers, and maintain escape routes from every situation. The safety behaviors meant to prevent panic actually maintained her vulnerability by confirming that panic was dangerous.

MCT for panic focuses on the meta-level – your relationship with panic rather than preventing panic sensations.

Attention training during panic: When panic begins, resist the urge to monitor symptoms or predict outcomes. Instead, use *external attention anchoring*. Choose five things you can see, four things you can hear, three things you can touch. This isn't distraction – it's appropriate attention allocation during a temporary physiological event.

Challenging panic beliefs: The key belief maintaining panic is: "Panic attacks are dangerous and must be prevented." Test this through graded exposure combined with metacognitive techniques. Instead of avoiding panic triggers, approach them while maintaining detached mindfulness toward panic sensations.

Post-panic attention control: After panic episodes, resist the urge to analyze what triggered it or how to prevent future attacks. This post-panic rumination maintains the disorder by keeping panic central in your attention. Use postponement: "I'll think about this during worry time if it's still relevant."

Studies show that **MCT reduces panic frequency by 85% within 8 weeks** compared to 45% for traditional CBT approaches (Wells & Papageorgiou, 2001). The difference lies in addressing the meta-level fear rather than just panic symptoms.

OCD and Intrusive Thoughts

OCD involves getting trapped in loops between intrusive thoughts and compulsive responses. The metacognitive element isn't the intrusive thoughts themselves – everyone has strange, unwanted thoughts – but your beliefs about these thoughts and your responsibility to control them.

The metacognitive model identifies three crucial beliefs that maintain OCD:

1. "Having this thought means something important about me"
2. "I must control or neutralize these thoughts"
3. "If I don't act on these thoughts, something terrible will happen"

Tom experienced intrusive thoughts about harm coming to his family. Instead of dismissing these as meaningless mental noise, he interpreted them as warnings requiring action. This led to checking behaviors, mental rituals, and avoidance that consumed hours daily while actually increasing the frequency and intensity of intrusive thoughts.

MCT treats intrusive thoughts as mental events requiring no response whatsoever.

Detached mindfulness for intrusive thoughts: When intrusive thoughts arise, practice the *mental radio* technique. Treat thoughts like stations on a radio – you can hear them without tuning in or changing channels. The thought "What if I hurt someone?" gets the same response as "What if it rains?" – acknowledgment without engagement.

Eliminating thought-action fusion: OCD often involves believing that thinking something increases the likelihood of it happening. Challenge this through *thought-action separation exercises*. Think deliberately about neutral unlikely events (finding money, meeting celebrities) and observe that thinking about them doesn't make them happen.

Response postponement: Instead of performing compulsions immediately, postpone them. Tell yourself: "I'll do this checking ritual in 10 minutes if it still seems necessary." Gradually extend postponement periods. Research shows that **95% of compulsive urges naturally diminish within 15 minutes** when not acted upon (Franklin & Foa, 2007).

Ritual elimination through attention control: Rather than fighting the urge to perform rituals, redirect attention to external tasks. When compulsive urges arise, immediately engage in activities requiring external attention – calling someone, reading aloud, or physical exercise.

PTSD and Trauma-Related Rumination

PTSD involves metacognitive patterns that maintain trauma symptoms long after the original event. The key isn't processing the trauma differently but changing how you respond to trauma-related thoughts and memories when they arise.

Post-trauma rumination typically involves two patterns:

1. **Why-focused rumination**: "Why did this happen to me? What could I have done differently?"
2. **Consequence rumination**: "How has this changed me? Will I ever feel normal again?"

Both patterns keep trauma central in awareness and prevent natural recovery processes from occurring.

MCT approaches trauma through attention control rather than memory processing. The goal isn't to eliminate trauma memories but to stop feeding them with ruminative attention.

Trauma-informed attention training: Standard attention training can feel overwhelming for trauma survivors. Modify the technique by starting with shorter periods (5 minutes instead of 12) and using gentler sounds. Focus on building attention control as a foundation for other trauma recovery work.

Memory intrusion management: When trauma memories intrude, use *memory surfing* – allow the memory to exist without engaging with its content or meaning. Treat memories like weather passing through – observable but not requiring analysis or response.

Rumination interruption: Trauma rumination often feels productive ("I need to understand what happened") but actually maintains symptoms. Apply postponement specifically to why-questions and consequence-analysis. Most trauma rumination involves problems that can't be solved through thinking, making postponement particularly effective.

Future-focused attention rebuilding: PTSD often damages future-oriented thinking. Use attention training to practice *forward attention* – deliberately focusing on upcoming positive events, goals, and possibilities. This rebuilds the capacity for future-focused awareness that trauma often disrupts.

Research indicates that **MCT reduces PTSD symptoms by 78% compared to 52% for trauma-focused CBT** (Wells & Colbear, 2012). The approach allows natural recovery processes to operate without interference from metacognitive patterns that maintain trauma symptoms.

Customizing Techniques for Your Specific Needs

Every anxiety pattern requires slight modifications to core MCT techniques. The key is identifying your particular version of the Cognitive Attentional Syndrome and adapting accordingly.

Assessment framework: Start by mapping your personal CAS pattern. What triggers your worry cycles? What specific thoughts capture your attention? Which beliefs about thinking maintain your patterns? What behaviors do you use to manage worry that actually make it worse?

Technique customization guidelines:

For **worry-dominant patterns** (GAD, health anxiety): Emphasize worry postponement and attention training. Practice external attention anchoring during high-worry periods.

For **attention-focused patterns** (social anxiety, panic): Prioritize attention redirecting techniques and detached mindfulness. Build external attention skills through structured practice.

For **rumination-dominant patterns** (depression, PTSD): Focus on rumination interruption and future-oriented attention training. Use postponement specifically for why-questions and analysis.

For **intrusion-dominant patterns** (OCD): Emphasize detached mindfulness and response postponement. Build tolerance for uncertainty without checking or neutralizing.

Progressive difficulty scheduling: Start with your easiest anxiety triggers and work toward more challenging situations. This builds confidence in MCT techniques before applying them to your most difficult patterns.

Integration timing: Don't try to apply all techniques simultaneously. Master attention training first (weeks 1-2), add detached mindfulness (weeks 3-4), then incorporate belief challenging (weeks 5-6). Each technique builds on previous ones.

When to Seek Professional Help

MCT self-help works for many people, but certain situations require professional guidance. You'll know it's time for additional support when self-guided practice isn't creating the changes you need.

Clear indicators for professional help:

Safety concerns: If you're having thoughts of self-harm, substance abuse to manage anxiety, or panic attacks that interfere with medical conditions, professional support becomes essential immediately.

Complexity factors: Multiple trauma histories, co-occurring eating disorders, bipolar disorder, or psychosis require specialized MCT adaptation that goes beyond self-help approaches.

Technique difficulties: If you can't establish basic attention training after 4 weeks of daily practice, or if detached mindfulness consistently increases rather than decreases distress, professional guidance can identify what's blocking progress.

Limited progress: After 8-10 weeks of consistent MCT practice, you should see measurable improvements in worry frequency and intensity. If anxiety levels remain unchanged, adding professional support can enhance your progress.

Finding qualified MCT practitioners: Look for therapists specifically trained in metacognitive therapy through Adrian Wells' institutes or certified MCT training programs. Many CBT therapists incorporate MCT techniques, but specialized MCT training provides the deepest expertise.

The International Association for Metacognitive Therapy (IAMCT) maintains directories of qualified practitioners. Initial sessions focus on metacognitive assessment and technique customization rather than extensive history-taking.

What to expect in MCT therapy: Professional MCT typically involves 8-12 sessions focusing on technique mastery and belief modification. Sessions emphasize practice rather than discussion, with significant homework assignments between meetings. The therapist helps identify your specific metacognitive patterns and adapts techniques accordingly.

Combining self-help with professional support: Many people benefit from using this book alongside professional MCT sessions. The book provides foundational understanding while therapy offers personalized guidance and troubleshooting for challenging situations.

Remember that seeking professional help represents wisdom, not failure. Some patterns require expert guidance to unravel effectively, and there's no shame in accessing additional support when needed.

Chapter 13: Depression, Rumination, and Finding Your Way Out

Depression creates one of the most persistent and damaging forms of mental loops: rumination. While anxiety typically focuses on future threats, depression traps you in past-focused thinking cycles that feel important but actually maintain hopelessness and despair.

Understanding how rumination maintains depression changes everything about recovery. Most approaches focus on changing thought content – thinking more positively or challenging negative thoughts. MCT reveals that the problem isn't what you're thinking about but that you're thinking in rumination mode at all.

Rumination feels productive because it masquerades as problem-solving. You convince yourself that analyzing past failures will prevent future ones, or that understanding why you feel depressed will somehow fix it. This creates what researchers call *depressive metacognitive beliefs* – the conviction that rumination is helpful, necessary, and meaningful.

The reality? **Rumination increases depression severity by 67% and doubles relapse risk** (Nolen-Hoeksema, 2000). Every minute spent in past-focused analysis deepens the depression rather than solving it.

The Rumination Trap in Depression

Depressive rumination typically follows predictable patterns. You replay past mistakes, analyze current problems endlessly, compare yourself to others, or try to figure out why you feel so low. These thinking patterns share common characteristics that maintain depression regardless of their specific content.

Pattern recognition:

- **Past-focused attention**: "Why did I mess up that relationship? What if I'd made different choices?"

- **Self-analytical loops**: "What's wrong with me? Why can't I just be happy like everyone else?"

- **Problem rehearsal**: "My life is falling apart. Nothing ever works out for me."

- **Comparative analysis**: "Everyone else has it figured out. I'm so far behind."

David's rumination centered on career disappointments. He'd spend hours analyzing past job decisions, comparing his progress to former colleagues, and trying to understand why his career felt stagnant. The more he analyzed, the more evidence he found for his failure, creating deeper depression that made career progress even more difficult.

The rumination-depression cycle: Rumination → Increased negative mood → More material for rumination → Deeper depression → Enhanced rumination. This cycle becomes self-perpetuating because rumination actually creates the very problems it claims to solve.

Why rumination feels so compelling: Depression makes rumination feel necessary and meaningful. You believe that if you just think hard enough, you'll figure out solutions or understand what's wrong. This belief keeps you trapped in thinking mode when what you actually need is to step out of thinking altogether.

Breaking the Past-Focused Thinking Cycle

The key to breaking depressive rumination isn't changing what you think about the past but changing your relationship with past-focused thinking entirely. MCT teaches you to recognize rumination as a mental activity that maintains depression rather than solving it.

Rumination vs. problem-solving: Learn to distinguish between productive problem-solving and depressive rumination. Problem-solving is specific, solution-focused, and time-limited. Rumination is general, emotion-focused, and endless. When you catch yourself ruminating, ask: "Is this helping me take specific action, or am I just going in circles?"

The rumination stop technique: When you notice rumination starting, use the *mental brake* approach. Tell yourself: "This is rumination, not problem-solving. I'm stepping out of this thinking mode now." Then immediately redirect attention to external activity.

Past-event postponement: Apply postponement specifically to past-focused thoughts. When your mind wants to replay past events or analyze past decisions, say: "I'll think about this during designated rumination time if it's still important." Schedule 15 minutes weekly for legitimate past-event review, but restrict it to specific problem-solving rather than general analysis.

Breaking analytical loops: Depression convinces you that self-analysis will lead to insights that solve problems. Challenge this by setting analysis time limits. Give yourself 5 minutes to analyze a situation, then stop regardless of whether you've reached conclusions. Most analysis beyond 5 minutes becomes repetitive rumination.

Attention redirecting for depression: Use external attention activities specifically chosen to counter depression's inward focus. Reading aloud, describing your environment in detail, or engaging in activities requiring external attention breaks the ruminative trance that maintains depressed mood.

Rebuilding Motivation Through Attention Control

Depression depletes motivation by keeping attention focused on problems, failures, and negative possibilities. MCT rebuilds motivation by teaching you to direct attention toward activities and goals rather than letting it get trapped in depressive thinking patterns.

The attention-motivation connection: What you pay attention to shapes how you feel and what actions seem possible. Depression directs attention to evidence of hopelessness while filtering out opportunities and positive possibilities. Attention training restores balance by giving you control over where your mental spotlight points.

Future-focused attention rebuilding: Practice deliberately focusing on upcoming events, potential opportunities, and forward-looking possibilities. This isn't positive thinking – it's attention training using future-oriented content instead of past-focused rumination.

Start small with tomorrow's activities, then expand to weekly plans, monthly goals, and longer-term possibilities. The key is attention practice, not necessarily believing in positive outcomes initially.

Activity-based attention training: Choose activities that naturally direct attention outward and forward. Physical exercise, creative projects, social interactions, and learning new skills all provide structured attention training that counters depression's inward focus.

Motivation through attention regulation: Instead of waiting to feel motivated before taking action, use action to train attention, which then rebuilds motivation. This reverses depression's typical pattern where low motivation prevents activity that would improve mood.

Research shows that **attention training alone reduces depression scores by 43%** before adding other MCT techniques (Siegle et al., 2007). Building attention control creates the foundation for other recovery activities to become possible and sustainable.

Combining MCT with Behavioral Activation

Behavioral activation complements MCT perfectly by providing structured activities that train attention while rebuilding positive reinforcement patterns. The combination addresses both the metacognitive maintenance of depression and the behavioral patterns that support recovery.

MCT-informed activity scheduling: Choose activities based on their attention-training value rather than just enjoyment potential. Activities requiring external focus and present-moment awareness provide dual benefits – they're inherently anti-ruminative while potentially increasing positive mood.

Attention-based activity selection: Prioritize activities that naturally redirect attention away from internal monitoring:

- **Social activities** that require interpersonal attention
- **Physical activities** that demand bodily awareness and coordination
- **Creative projects** that require problem-solving and external focus
- **Learning activities** that engage curiosity and forward-thinking
- **Service activities** that direct attention toward others' needs

Rumination-proofing your activity practice: Depression often turns positive activities into rumination triggers. You might exercise while analyzing your problems or socialize while monitoring your mood. Practice *pure attention* during activities – engaging fully without meta-analysis of how the activity affects your depression.

Progress tracking without rumination: Track behavioral activation progress through simple activity completion rather than mood analysis. This prevents turning positive activities into depression-analysis opportunities while maintaining accountability for activity engagement.

Success Stories of Depression Recovery

Real recovery stories illustrate how MCT principles work in practice. These examples show the progression from rumination-dominated depression to attention-controlled recovery.

Maria's story: Maria spent months analyzing why her marriage ended, what she could have done differently, and what this meant about her worth as a person. MCT helped her recognize this analysis as rumination maintaining depression rather than healing it. She learned to postpone past-relationship analysis and redirect attention to present-moment activities and future possibilities. Within 6 weeks, her depression lifted enough to allow actual problem-solving about her new life situation.

James's breakthrough: James ruminated about career failures and financial setbacks, convincing himself that understanding his mistakes would prevent future ones. MCT showed him that this analysis was keeping him stuck in problem-focused thinking rather than solution-focused action. He learned to limit analysis time and direct attention toward job search activities and skill development. His motivation returned as his attention shifted from past failures to future possibilities.

Key recovery patterns:

1. **Recognition phase**: Learning to identify rumination as it begins rather than getting lost in content

2. **Interruption phase**: Developing skills to stop rumination and redirect attention

3. **Rebuilding phase**: Using attention control to engage in recovery-supporting activities

4. **Maintenance phase**: Preventing rumination relapse through ongoing attention training

Timeline expectations: Most people notice rumination reduction within 2-3 weeks of consistent MCT practice. Mood improvements typically follow attention improvements by 1-2 weeks. Full recovery patterns establish within 6-12 weeks of regular technique application.

Creating Your Personal Anti-Rumination Plan

Effective depression recovery requires a customized approach that addresses your specific rumination patterns while building sustainable attention control habits.

Rumination pattern identification: Track your rumination themes for one week. Notice whether you ruminate about past events, current problems, self-analysis, or comparative thinking. Each pattern requires slightly different MCT applications.

Daily structure development: Create daily routines that naturally limit rumination opportunities while providing structured attention training. Morning attention practice, scheduled activity periods, and evening wind-down routines create framework that supports recovery.

Environmental modification: Identify physical environments that trigger rumination and modify them when possible. This might mean changing where you spend unstructured time, reducing social media access, or creating dedicated spaces for attention training practice.

Support system integration: Teach family members and friends to recognize your rumination patterns and how to respond helpfully. They can learn to redirect conversations away from analysis and toward present-moment or future-focused topics.

Relapse prevention planning: Develop specific plans for handling rumination resurgence during stressful periods. This includes early warning sign recognition, technique intensification protocols, and professional support access plans.

Long-term maintenance: Plan for ongoing attention training beyond initial recovery. Regular attention practice prevents rumination patterns from re-establishing during future difficult periods.

The research consistently demonstrates that **MCT for depression shows 74% recovery rates compared to 46% for traditional CBT** (Papageorgiou & Wells, 2003). The key difference lies in targeting the metacognitive processes that maintain depression rather than just challenging negative thought content.

Chapter 14: MCT in Relationships and Daily Life

MCT principles transform more than just your internal mental experience – they revolutionize how you navigate relationships, work challenges, and daily stressors. When you understand how attention and metacognitive beliefs operate in interpersonal situations, you gain tools for improving every area of your life.

The beauty of MCT lies in its universal applicability. The same attention control skills that reduce anxiety also improve listening ability. The detached mindfulness that stops rumination also prevents relationship conflicts from escalating. The postponement that manages worry also creates space for thoughtful responses in challenging situations.

Most relationship problems involve attention and metacognitive elements. We monitor our partner's mood, ruminate about relationship issues, worry about future problems, and maintain beliefs about what good relationships require. These patterns create exactly the relationship difficulties we're trying to prevent.

Teaching MCT Concepts to Family Members

Sharing MCT with loved ones creates mutual support while improving family dynamics. However, teaching these concepts requires finesse – people need to discover MCT benefits naturally rather than feeling lectured or fixed.

Starting conversations about thinking patterns: Begin by sharing your own experience rather than analyzing others' patterns. "I've been learning about how attention works, and it's been really helpful for my worry" opens dialogue without creating defensiveness.

The contagion effect: When you stop engaging with family rumination and worry cycles, others often naturally follow. Your detached mindfulness during family stress demonstrates alternative responses without requiring explanation or justification.

Teaching attention awareness: Help family members notice their attention patterns through gentle observation rather than correction. "I notice we're all focused on this problem right now. What if we took a break and came back to it later?" models attention flexibility without criticism.

Family worry postponement: Establish family policies about worry discussions. Create designated times for problem-solving while postponing worry conversations during meals, family time, or before bed. This protects family time while ensuring important issues get attention.

Sarah's family implemented "worry-free dinner" policy after learning MCT principles. They postponed problem discussions until after dinner, allowing family connection time without stress-focused conversation. Problem-solving discussions became more productive when scheduled rather than happening randomly during family time.

Modeling metacognitive flexibility: Demonstrate MCT principles through your responses to family stress rather than teaching them explicitly. Your calm responses to family chaos, your refusal to engage in rumination cycles, and your attention to present-moment family experiences teach more effectively than explanations.

Supporting without enabling: Learn to support family members without joining their worry cycles. You can care about someone's problems without engaging in rumination about them. Offer comfort and practical help while maintaining detached mindfulness about outcomes you can't control.

Handling Others' Resistance to Your Changes

When you change your metacognitive patterns, family and friends often experience discomfort. They're used to you worrying with them, analyzing problems together, or maintaining certain relationship dynamics. Your new MCT behaviors can feel strange or even threatening to people who rely on your old patterns.

Understanding resistance sources: People resist your changes for various reasons. Some enjoy having a worry partner who validates their concerns. Others interpret your detached mindfulness as not caring. Some feel abandoned when you stop engaging in their rumination cycles.

Communicating changes clearly: Explain your new approach directly: "I'm learning to handle worry differently. I still care about this problem, but I'm not going to spend hours analyzing it because that doesn't actually help." This prevents misinterpretation of your MCT practices as indifference.

Maintaining relationships while protecting your progress: You can stay connected with people while refusing to engage in their CAS patterns. Use phrases like: "I can see this is really bothering you. What specific action might help?" This redirects from rumination to problem-solving while showing continued care.

Setting metacognitive boundaries: Learn to say: "I don't want to spend time analyzing this right now" or "Let's take a break from this topic and come back to it later." These boundaries protect your attention while maintaining relationships.

When others try to pull you into worry cycles: Family and friends might persist in trying to engage you in worry discussions. Maintain your boundaries consistently: "I care about you, and I'm not going to worry about this with you because worry doesn't help either of us."

The ripple effect: Often, your consistent MCT practice eventually influences others positively. They begin to notice that your approach reduces stress without reducing care, leading them to naturally adopt similar patterns.

MCT for Parenting and Family Stress

Parenting creates unique challenges for attention control and worry management. You're responsible for another person's wellbeing while trying to maintain your own mental health. MCT provides frameworks for responsive parenting without falling into anxiety traps.

Parental worry management: Distinguish between productive parental concern and unproductive parental rumination. Productive concern leads to specific protective actions. Rumination involves endless analysis of potential dangers without clear action steps.

Apply postponement to parental what-if scenarios: "What if something happens at school? What if they make bad friend choices? What if they don't succeed academically?" Schedule specific times for parenting concern review rather than maintaining constant vigilance.

Attention training while parenting: Use parenting activities as attention training opportunities. When playing with children, reading stories, or helping with homework, practice complete external attention focus. This improves both your attention control and your parenting quality.

Teaching children metacognitive awareness: Help children recognize their own worry and rumination patterns without creating anxiety about anxiety. Use simple language: "Sometimes our brains get stuck thinking about problems over and over. Let's do something else for a while and see if the problem gets clearer later."

Family stress management: When family crises arise, apply MCT principles to maintain clear thinking. Use attention control to focus on specific action steps rather than getting lost in crisis rumination. Model calm response patterns that children can learn from.

Parental guilt and rumination: Parenting often triggers rumination about mistakes, comparisons to other parents, and analysis of children's problems. Apply postponement to parental analysis: "I'll think about this parenting decision during my scheduled worry time if it's still important."

School and activity stress: Help children apply simple MCT concepts to academic and social pressures. Teach attention focusing for studying, worry postponement for test anxiety, and detached mindfulness for social situations.

Workplace Applications and Career Benefits

MCT principles provide significant advantages in professional settings by improving focus, decision-making, and stress management. The attention control skills that reduce anxiety also enhance work performance and career satisfaction.

Meeting and presentation anxiety: Apply social anxiety MCT techniques to professional situations. Use external attention anchoring during presentations, postpone pre-meeting worry, and practice detached mindfulness toward performance monitoring thoughts.

Workplace rumination management: Work stress often triggers rumination about deadlines, colleague relationships, or career progress. Apply postponement to work worry outside of business hours. Designate specific times for career analysis rather than allowing it to infiltrate all aspects of life.

Decision-making improvement: MCT improves decision-making by reducing the rumination that clouds judgment. When facing career choices, apply postponement to repetitive analysis and use attention training to gather information systematically rather than getting lost in endless consideration.

Conflict resolution: Use detached mindfulness during workplace conflicts to maintain perspective and respond thoughtfully rather than reactively. This prevents escalation while protecting your own mental state during challenging interpersonal situations.

Productivity enhancement: Attention training directly improves work focus and productivity. The same skills that redirect attention from worry also help maintain concentration during complex work tasks.

Jennifer applied MCT principles to law firm stress. She learned to postpone case worry outside work hours, use attention training during document review, and apply detached mindfulness during client meetings. Her billable hour productivity increased by 23% while her work-related anxiety decreased significantly.

Career development through attention control: Use attention training to focus on skill development rather than getting trapped in career analysis rumination. Direct attention toward learning opportunities, networking activities, and goal-oriented actions rather than endless consideration of career paths.

Academic and Test Anxiety Applications

Academic environments trigger multiple anxiety patterns that MCT addresses effectively. Test anxiety, performance monitoring, comparative thinking, and future-focused worry all respond well to metacognitive interventions.

Pre-exam worry management: Apply postponement to test-related what-if scenarios while maintaining appropriate study preparation.

The goal isn't eliminating all exam concern but preventing worry from interfering with effective preparation.

Study attention training: Use academic work as attention training practice. When studying, practice complete focus on material without monitoring comprehension or predicting performance. This improves both learning and attention control.

Test-taking attention control: During exams, use attention anchoring to maintain focus on questions rather than monitoring anxiety or predicting outcomes. When anxiety thoughts arise, redirect to the specific exam content requiring attention.

Academic rumination prevention: Students often ruminate about grades, comparing performance to others, or analyzing study methods. Apply postponement to academic analysis outside of scheduled study review periods.

Performance anxiety in academic settings: Apply social anxiety MCT techniques to classroom participation, presentations, and group work. Use external attention focus rather than self-monitoring during academic performance situations.

Research indicates that **MCT reduces test anxiety by 68% while improving academic performance by 15%** (Spada et al., 2008). The attention control skills transfer directly to improved learning and academic achievement.

Building an MCT-Informed Lifestyle

Integrating MCT principles into daily life creates a sustainable approach to mental health that goes beyond technique practice. This involves designing your environment, relationships, and routines to support metacognitive health.

Environmental design for attention control: Create physical spaces that support external attention focus. Reduce clutter that triggers monitoring or rumination. Design work and living spaces that naturally direct attention outward rather than inward.

Information diet management: Apply MCT principles to media consumption. Notice how news, social media, and entertainment affect your attention patterns. Reduce information sources that trigger rumination or worry cycles while maintaining appropriate awareness of important information.

Social environment curation: Choose relationships and social activities that support your MCT practice. Limit time with people who consistently engage in rumination or worry cycles. Seek relationships that naturally encourage present-moment awareness and future-focused thinking.

Routine integration: Build MCT techniques into daily routines so they become automatic rather than effortful. Morning attention training, commute worry postponement, and evening reflection time create structure that maintains metacognitive health.

Stress response preparation: Develop protocols for applying MCT during predictable stress situations. Know in advance how you'll respond to work deadlines, family crises, health concerns, or financial pressures using MCT principles.

Long-term lifestyle maintenance: Plan for maintaining MCT practices during life changes, increased stress periods, or busy seasons. This prevents gradual return to old metacognitive patterns when life becomes challenging.

The goal isn't perfection but building a lifestyle that naturally supports healthy metacognitive patterns while providing tools for managing inevitable stress and challenges.

Chapter 15: Frequently Asked Questions and Troubleshooting

After working with thousands of people learning MCT techniques, certain questions come up repeatedly. These concerns often reflect normal struggles with implementing a new approach to mental health, and addressing them directly helps prevent abandoning MCT practice when it's most needed.

These questions reveal common misconceptions about how MCT works and what results to expect. Understanding these issues prevents frustration and helps you navigate the learning process more effectively.

"What if I can't stop worrying about real problems?"

This question reflects one of the most common misunderstandings about MCT. The approach isn't about ignoring real problems or stopping all concern about genuine issues. MCT teaches you to distinguish between productive problem-solving and unproductive worry cycles.

Real problems vs. worry loops: Real problems have potential solutions and benefit from focused attention. Worry loops involve repetitive thinking about problems without reaching solutions or taking action. The key is learning which thinking patterns actually help solve problems and which ones just create more distress.

The worry effectiveness test: When you catch yourself worrying about a "real problem," ask these questions: Is this worry leading to specific action? Am I learning anything new about this problem?

Am I getting closer to a solution? If the answers are no, you're in a worry loop rather than productive problem-solving.

Productive concern vs. unproductive rumination: Productive concern is time-limited, solution-focused, and leads to action. You think about the problem long enough to develop an action plan, then redirect attention to implementing solutions. Unproductive rumination continues indefinitely without reaching actionable conclusions.

Scheduled problem-solving time: For genuine problems requiring attention, schedule specific problem-solving periods. Give yourself 15-30 minutes to focus completely on the issue, generate potential solutions, and decide on next steps. Outside these scheduled times, postpone further thinking about the problem.

Action-oriented worry: Transform worry into action wherever possible. Instead of worrying about job security, update your resume. Instead of worrying about health, schedule medical checkups. Instead of worrying about relationships, plan quality time with loved ones.

Research shows that **83% of worry topics never require the action that worry suggests is necessary** (Borkovec et al., 1998). Most worry involves problems that either resolve themselves or can't be solved through thinking.

When problems genuinely need attention: Some situations genuinely require ongoing attention and concern. Financial difficulties, health issues, relationship conflicts, and work challenges deserve appropriate attention. MCT helps you give these situations the right amount and type of attention without getting trapped in worry cycles that make problems worse.

"How is this different from just distraction?"

This question highlights an important distinction that determines whether MCT techniques work effectively. MCT isn't distraction or avoidance – it's attention training that changes your relationship with thoughts and worries.

Distraction vs. attention training: Distraction involves avoiding thoughts or feelings by keeping busy. Attention training involves developing skills to direct attention flexibly while remaining aware of thoughts and feelings without getting trapped by them.

When you use distraction, you're running away from thoughts. When you use MCT attention techniques, you're learning to coexist with thoughts without being controlled by them.

The awareness difference: MCT maintains awareness of thoughts while changing how you respond to them. You notice worry thoughts arising but choose not to engage with their content. Distraction tries to avoid noticing thoughts altogether.

Skill building vs. avoidance: MCT builds long-term skills for managing any type of mental content. Distraction provides temporary relief but doesn't develop lasting capabilities for handling difficult thoughts or situations.

Flexibility vs. rigidity: MCT creates flexible attention control – you can choose to engage with thoughts when it's helpful and choose not to engage when it's unproductive. Distraction creates rigid avoidance patterns that limit your response options.

The engagement continuum: MCT teaches you that you have multiple options for responding to thoughts: complete engagement, partial engagement, detached observation, or temporary postponement. Distraction only offers the option of avoidance.

Building tolerance vs. building dependence: MCT builds tolerance for uncertainty and difficult emotions by teaching you that you don't need to respond to every mental event. Distraction builds dependence on external activities to manage internal states.

"Can I combine MCT with medication?"

MCT works effectively both independently and in combination with psychiatric medications. The two approaches target different aspects of anxiety and depression, making them highly compatible.

Complementary mechanisms: Medications often address neurotransmitter imbalances that contribute to anxiety and depression. MCT addresses the metacognitive patterns that maintain these conditions. Combining both approaches can provide comprehensive treatment.

Medication as attention training support: Some people find that medication reduces baseline anxiety enough to make attention training practice easier initially. As MCT skills develop, some individuals choose to work with prescribers to reduce medication gradually.

Timing considerations: Starting MCT while on stable medication often works well. Avoid making medication changes during initial MCT learning periods to avoid confusing the source of improvements or difficulties.

Communication with prescribers: Inform your prescriber about MCT practice. Many psychiatrists and primary care physicians appreciate patients learning self-regulation skills that complement medical treatment.

Medication-assisted attention training: If anxiety or depression significantly impairs concentration, medication might improve your ability to practice attention training initially. This can accelerate MCT learning and create positive feedback cycles.

Research demonstrates that **combined MCT and medication treatment shows 89% response rates compared to 71% for medication alone** (Wells et al., 2010). The combination appears to provide benefits beyond either approach individually.

Withdrawal consideration: If you choose to reduce medications while practicing MCT, work closely with your prescriber to develop gradual tapering schedules. MCT skills can support medication reduction but shouldn't replace medical guidance about withdrawal timing and methods.

"What if the techniques make me feel worse initially?"

This concern reflects a normal part of learning any new mental health approach. MCT can initially feel uncomfortable because you're changing habitual patterns that your brain has used for protection, even when those patterns weren't actually helping.

Normal adjustment reactions: When you first stop engaging with worry thoughts, anxiety might temporarily increase. Your brain interprets this as danger: "If you're not worrying about this, something bad will happen!" This reaction typically lasts 1-3 weeks as your brain adjusts to new response patterns.

The extinction burst phenomenon: Psychology research shows that when you stop reinforcing a behavior (like responding to worry thoughts), the behavior often increases temporarily before decreasing. This *extinction burst* is actually a sign that change is beginning.

Why techniques might feel wrong initially: MCT asks you to do the opposite of what anxiety demands. Instead of analyzing threats, you postpone worry. Instead of monitoring symptoms, you redirect attention. Instead of solving problems through thinking, you step out of thinking mode. These responses feel counterintuitive initially.

Building tolerance gradually: Start with less threatening situations to build confidence in MCT techniques. Practice attention training during low-stress periods before applying it during high-anxiety moments. This creates positive associations with techniques before using them in challenging situations.

Monitoring progress appropriately: Track progress through behavior changes rather than immediate feeling changes. Notice whether you're worrying less frequently or for shorter periods, even if anxiety intensity hasn't decreased yet. Attention changes typically precede mood changes by several weeks.

When to persist vs. when to modify: Persist with techniques if you notice any positive changes in thinking patterns, even if anxiety levels remain high initially. Modify approaches if techniques consistently increase distress after 3-4 weeks of regular practice, or if you're unable to implement basic attention training.

Professional support for difficult adjustments: If initial increases in anxiety feel overwhelming or interfere with daily functioning, professional MCT guidance can help navigate the adjustment period more comfortably while maintaining progress toward improvement.

Integration with Other Therapy Approaches

MCT combines effectively with many other therapeutic approaches while maintaining its distinct focus on metacognitive processes. Understanding how MCT fits with other treatments helps you make informed decisions about comprehensive care.

MCT and traditional CBT: MCT differs from CBT by focusing on how you think rather than what you think. While CBT challenges specific thought content, MCT teaches you to change your relationship with thoughts altogether. Many people benefit from CBT's practical coping strategies combined with MCT's attention control techniques.

MCT and acceptance-based approaches: ACT (Acceptance and Commitment Therapy) and MCT share emphasis on changing relationships with thoughts rather than changing thought content. MCT's detached mindfulness aligns well with ACT's psychological flexibility concepts. The approaches complement each other while MCT provides more specific attention training protocols.

MCT and mindfulness meditation: Traditional mindfulness meditation and MCT both involve attention training, but with different goals. Mindfulness meditation aims for present-moment awareness and acceptance. MCT aims for flexible attention control and reduced engagement with CAS patterns. Many people practice both approaches successfully.

MCT and trauma therapy: For trauma-related anxiety and PTSD, MCT often works well alongside trauma-focused therapies like EMDR or trauma-focused CBT. MCT addresses the rumination and worry patterns that maintain trauma symptoms, while trauma-focused approaches address the trauma memories themselves.

MCT and interpersonal therapy: Relationship-focused therapy approaches combine well with MCT because attention control and detached mindfulness improve interpersonal functioning. MCT provides tools for managing relationship anxiety while interpersonal therapy addresses relationship patterns directly.

Sequential vs. simultaneous integration: Some people benefit from learning MCT first, then adding other approaches. Others prefer simultaneous integration. The key is avoiding approach confusion – understanding which techniques come from which framework and how they work together.

Finding MCT Therapists and Resources

While this book provides comprehensive MCT self-help guidance, some situations benefit from professional MCT training and support.

Finding qualified MCT practitioners requires understanding what training and credentials indicate genuine expertise.

Credentialing and training standards: Look for therapists who completed formal MCT training through Adrian Wells' Greater Manchester programmes, the MCT Institute, or certified training centers. MCT requires specialized training beyond general CBT education.

Professional directories: The International Association for Metacognitive Therapy (IAMCT) maintains directories of certified MCT practitioners. These therapists have completed supervision requirements and demonstrated competency in MCT assessment and treatment.

What to ask potential therapists: "What specific MCT training have you completed?" "How many MCT cases have you treated?" "Do you use MCT as a primary approach or integrate it with other methods?" These questions help you find practitioners with genuine MCT expertise.

Online vs. in-person MCT: Research shows that **MCT works effectively through telehealth with comparable outcomes to in-person treatment** (Wells et al., 2021). This expands access to qualified MCT practitioners regardless of geographic location.

Cost and insurance considerations: MCT typically requires fewer sessions than traditional therapy approaches (8-12 sessions vs. 20+ sessions), potentially reducing overall treatment costs. Check whether your insurance covers therapy services and whether MCT practitioners accept your specific insurance plan.

Self-help vs. professional guidance: Use professional MCT support when self-help practice isn't creating desired changes, when you need help customizing techniques for complex situations, or when you want accelerated progress with expert guidance.

Advanced Training Opportunities

For people who want to deepen their MCT understanding beyond this book's scope, various advanced training opportunities provide additional education and skill development.

MCT practitioner training: Mental health professionals can pursue MCT certification through formal training programs. These programs provide comprehensive training in MCT theory, assessment, and treatment protocols.

Research participation: Universities conducting MCT research often seek participants for studies examining technique effectiveness. Participating in research provides access to expert guidance while contributing to scientific understanding of MCT approaches.

Continuing education workshops: Professional organizations offer MCT workshops and continuing education programs. These provide updates on latest research and advanced technique applications.

Online learning platforms: Several platforms offer MCT courses ranging from introductory overviews to advanced practitioner training. These provide flexible learning options for people wanting to deepen their understanding.

Reading and research: Adrian Wells' professional texts provide comprehensive MCT theory and research foundations. While more technical than this book, they offer detailed understanding of metacognitive assessment and treatment protocols.

Community and support groups: Online communities focused on MCT practice provide peer support and technique sharing. These groups help maintain motivation and provide troubleshooting assistance from others using MCT approaches.

The MCT approach continues evolving as research expands understanding of metacognitive processes and their role in psychological wellbeing. Staying connected with MCT developments ensures you have access to the most current and effective applications of these powerful techniques.

Remember: MCT isn't just a set of techniques – it's a new way of understanding how your mind works and how to work with your mind more effectively. The skills you develop through MCT practice create lasting changes that improve not just anxiety and depression but your overall quality of life and mental flexibility.

What You've Accomplished

You now have comprehensive understanding of how MCT applies to specific anxiety patterns, depression recovery, relationship challenges, and daily life situations. These advanced applications demonstrate MCT's versatility and power for creating lasting change across all areas of your experience.

The techniques you've learned work because they address the fundamental processes that maintain psychological distress. Whether you're dealing with social anxiety, depression rumination, family stress, or workplace challenges, the same metacognitive principles provide effective solutions.

Your journey with MCT extends far beyond managing anxiety and depression. These skills create foundations for resilience, improved relationships, enhanced performance, and greater life satisfaction. The attention control and metacognitive flexibility you develop become lifelong resources for navigating whatever challenges and opportunities arise.

Part V: Resources and Tools

This final section provides everything you need to implement MCT successfully in your daily life. Think of these resources as your MCT toolkit – practical guides, worksheets, and references that support your practice long after you've finished reading the main chapters.

The materials here aren't just add-ons to the book. They're designed to be your go-to resources when you need quick technique reminders, want to track your progress, or encounter situations that require immediate MCT application. Keep these pages accessible for regular reference.

You'll notice that these tools focus on action rather than analysis. That's intentional. MCT works through practice, not through endless reading about practice. These resources get you practicing effectively and efficiently.

Appendix A: Quick Reference Guides

When you're in the middle of a worry spiral or panic attack, you don't need lengthy explanations – you need immediate, actionable steps. These quick reference guides provide exactly that: clear, simple instructions for applying MCT techniques in real-time situations.

Technique Cheat Sheets

ATTENTION TRAINING TECHNIQUE (ATT) - 12-MINUTE VERSION

Setup (1 minute):

- Sit comfortably with eyes closed

- Identify three sound categories: close sounds, distant sounds, very distant sounds

- Begin with selective attention to one close sound

Phase 1 - Selective Attention (4 minutes):

- Minutes 1-2: Focus on one close sound (clock, fan, traffic)

- Minutes 3-4: Switch to one distant sound (neighborhood activity, HVAC)

- **If mind wanders:** Gently return attention to chosen sound

Phase 2 - Divided Attention (4 minutes):

- Minutes 5-6: Hold attention on two sounds simultaneously

- Minutes 7-8: Expand to three sounds at once

- **Goal:** Maintain awareness of multiple sounds without switching between them

Phase 3 - Flexible Attention (4 minutes):

- Minutes 9-10: Rapidly switch attention between different sounds every 15 seconds

- Minutes 11-12: Try to hear all sounds simultaneously, then focus on just one

- **End:** Slowly open eyes and notice your attention control

Common mistakes to avoid:

- Don't strain or force attention – use gentle focus

- Don't analyze sounds or create stories about them

- Don't worry about "doing it right" – practice builds skill over time

- Don't extend beyond 12 minutes initially

DETACHED MINDFULNESS QUICK GUIDE

The RAIN Approach:

- **R**ecognize: "I notice I'm having the thought that..."

- **A**llow: "This thought can be here without me engaging with it"

- **I**nvestigate: "What would happen if I just let this thought pass by?"

- **N**on-attachment: "I don't need to respond to this mental event"

Beach Ball Metaphor Application: When unwanted thoughts arise:

1. Imagine thoughts as beach balls floating in water

    2. You're observing from the shore, not in the water
    3. Let thoughts float by without grabbing them or pushing them away
    4. Your job is watching, not controlling what floats past

No Comment Technique:

- Thought arises: "What if I lose my job?"
- Response: "No comment" (internally)
- Redirect attention to current activity
- Repeat as often as necessary

Common detached mindfulness phrases:

- "That's just a thought"
- "Interesting that my mind went there"
- "No need to engage with this right now"
- "I can notice this without responding"
- "This is just mental activity"

WORRY POSTPONEMENT STEP-BY-STEP

Immediate Response (when worry starts):

1. **Notice** the worry beginning: "I'm starting to worry about..."
2. **Label** it as postponable: "This is worry, not emergency problem-solving"
3. **Postpone** with specific timing: "I'll think about this at 7 PM if it's still important"
4. **Redirect** attention to current activity immediately

5. **Record** the worry briefly if helpful (optional)

Designated Worry Time Setup:

- **Duration:** 15-20 minutes maximum
- **Timing:** Same time daily, not within 3 hours of bedtime
- **Location:** Specific chair or location, not bed or relaxation areas
- **Rules:** Focus only on worries that still feel important; discard any that seem irrelevant

What happens during worry time:

- Review postponed worries from your list
- Spend maximum 3 minutes per worry topic
- Focus on actionable solutions, not endless analysis
- Many postponed worries will feel unimportant by worry time
- End promptly after 15-20 minutes regardless of completion

BELIEF CHALLENGING QUICK REFERENCE

Identifying Problematic Beliefs:

- "I must worry to be prepared"
- "Worrying shows I care"
- "If I don't worry, bad things will happen"
- "I can't control my thoughts"
- "Rumination helps me understand myself"
- "Monitoring my anxiety prevents panic"

Quick Belief Testing:

1. **Question:** "Is this belief actually true?"
2. **Evidence:** "What evidence supports/contradicts this belief?"
3. **Experiment:** "What would happen if I acted as if this belief were false?"
4. **Alternative:** "What would be a more helpful belief?"

Behavioral Experiment Framework:

- **Prediction:** "If I don't worry about X, then Y will happen"
- **Test:** Deliberately don't worry for specified time period
- **Observation:** "What actually happened?"
- **Conclusion:** "What does this tell me about my belief?"

Emergency Protocols for Crisis Moments

Crisis situations require immediate attention control rather than lengthy technique application. These protocols provide structured responses for panic attacks, overwhelming anxiety, severe rumination episodes, and other mental health emergencies.

PANIC ATTACK PROTOCOL

Immediate Response (first 60 seconds):

1. **Recognize:** "This is panic, not danger"
2. **Breathe:** Normal breathing, don't force deep breaths
3. **Anchor:** Name 5 things you can see right now
4. **Stay:** Don't flee the situation unless actually dangerous
5. **Wait:** Panic peaks within 5-10 minutes, then naturally decreases

Extended Response (minutes 2-10):

- Continue external attention anchoring (sounds, textures, sights)
- Resist urge to monitor heart rate or analyze symptoms
- Use mantra: "This is temporary and not dangerous"
- Focus on immediate environment rather than internal sensations
- Remember: Fighting panic makes it worse, accepting it makes it pass

Post-Panic Recovery:

- Resist urge to analyze what triggered the attack
- Don't make major decisions immediately after panic
- Return to normal activities as soon as safely possible
- Postpone panic analysis until scheduled worry time
- Credit yourself for surviving another false alarm

OVERWHELMING ANXIETY CRISIS PROTOCOL

Immediate Stabilization:

1. **Ground physically:** Feel your feet on floor, hands on surfaces
2. **Name your location:** "I'm in my kitchen, it's Tuesday afternoon"
3. **Breathe normally:** Don't force deep breathing if it increases anxiety
4. **Move slowly:** Gentle movement, avoid rapid actions that increase arousal

5. **Limit decisions:** Postpone all non-essential decisions until anxiety decreases

Attention Recovery Steps:

- Choose one specific external focus point (clock, tree outside, specific sound)
- Maintain attention on chosen focus for 2-3 minutes minimum
- When attention drifts to worry, gently return to external focus
- Gradually expand attention to include broader environment
- Avoid analyzing why anxiety increased or predicting when it will end

SEVERE RUMINATION EPISODE PROTOCOL

Rumination Circuit Breaker:

1. **Stop physical position:** If sitting/lying down ruminating, stand up immediately
2. **Change location:** Move to different room or go outside
3. **Engage body:** Physical movement, stretching, or exercise
4. **External task:** Call someone, read aloud, organize something
5. **Time limit:** Set 30-minute timer for current activity before reassessing

Rumination Emergency Phrases:

- "This thinking is making things worse, not better"
- "I'm going in circles instead of solving anything"

- "My brain is stuck in analysis mode"
- "Time to step out of thinking and into action"
- "This problem will still exist later if it needs attention"

Crisis Support Decision Tree:

- **If having thoughts of self-harm:** Contact crisis hotline or emergency services immediately
- **If unable to function:** Contact trusted friend, family member, or mental health professional
- **If techniques aren't helping:** Use crisis protocols, then seek same-day professional support
- **If situation feels manageable:** Apply emergency protocols and schedule follow-up support within 24 hours

Daily Practice Schedules

Consistency builds MCT skills more effectively than intensity. These schedules provide structured approaches for integrating MCT practice into daily routines without creating additional stress or time pressure.

BEGINNER SCHEDULE (Weeks 1-2)

Morning Routine (10 minutes):

- 5 minutes: Attention training (shortened version)
- 3 minutes: Daily intention setting (what will you focus on today?)
- 2 minutes: Quick body awareness without monitoring

Midday Check-in (5 minutes):

- Brief attention reset (focus on immediate environment)

- Worry postponement for any morning concerns
- Redirect attention to afternoon priorities

Evening Practice (15 minutes):

- 12 minutes: Full attention training technique
- 3 minutes: Detached mindfulness practice with any day's stress

Weekly Goals:

- Establish consistent practice timing
- Learn basic attention control skills
- Begin recognizing worry and rumination patterns
- Practice worry postponement 3-5 times daily

INTERMEDIATE SCHEDULE (Weeks 3-6)

Morning Foundation (15 minutes):

- 12 minutes: Full attention training technique
- 3 minutes: Intention setting with attention goals

Workday Applications:

- Use transitional moments for mini-attention training (between meetings, before phone calls)
- Apply worry postponement to work stress immediately when it arises
- Practice detached mindfulness during challenging interactions

Evening Integration (20 minutes):

- 15 minutes: Designated worry time (if needed) or extended attention training
- 5 minutes: Day review focusing on successful MCT applications

Weekly Goals:

- Integrate techniques into daily activities seamlessly
- Reduce worry frequency and duration measurably
- Apply detached mindfulness to interpersonal situations
- Begin behavioral experiments with metacognitive beliefs

ADVANCED SCHEDULE (Week 7+)

Flexible Daily Practice:

- **Core practice:** 12-minute attention training (morning or evening)
- **Situational applications:** MCT techniques applied to real-life situations as they arise
- **Weekly review:** 30 minutes analyzing progress and adjusting technique applications

Maintenance Focus:

- Attention training becomes automatic background skill
- Techniques applied spontaneously during challenging situations
- Focus shifts to preventing old pattern relapse
- Integration of MCT principles into lifestyle and relationship patterns

Progress Tracking Templates

Effective progress tracking focuses on behavior changes rather than mood monitoring. These templates help you notice improvements in worry frequency, rumination duration, and attention control without creating additional self-monitoring problems.

WEEKLY PRACTICE TRACKING

Attention Training Log:

Week of: _____

Monday: ATT completed? Y/N Duration: ___ Quality (1-10): ___

Tuesday: ATT completed? Y/N Duration: ___ Quality (1-10): ___

Wednesday: ATT completed? Y/N Duration: ___ Quality (1-10): ___

Thursday: ATT completed? Y/N Duration: ___ Quality (1-10): ___

Friday: ATT completed? Y/N Duration: ___ Quality (1-10): ___

Saturday: ATT completed? Y/N Duration: ___ Quality (1-10): ___

Sunday: ATT completed? Y/N Duration: ___ Quality (1-10): ___

Notes about attention improvements this week:
_____

Worry Postponement Success Tracking:

Daily Worry Postponement Log

Date: _____

Morning worries postponed: _____ (number)

Afternoon worries postponed: _____ (number)

Evening worries postponed: _____ (number)

Percentage of postponed worries that still seemed important during worry time: ____%

Most successful postponement situation today:

_____

Most challenging postponement situation today:

_____

MONTHLY PROGRESS ASSESSMENT

Metacognitive Pattern Changes:

Month: _____

Rumination Frequency:

- Beginning of month: ___ times per day

- End of month: ___ times per day

Average Rumination Duration:

- Beginning of month: ___ minutes per episode

- End of month: ___ minutes per episode

Worry Intensity (1-10 scale):

- Beginning of month: ___

- End of month: ___

Attention Control Improvement:

- Can maintain focus during conversations: Y/N

- Can redirect from worry thoughts: Y/N

- Can practice detached mindfulness during stress: Y/N

Biggest improvement this month:

_____

Area needing more focus next month:

_____

SITUATIONAL APPLICATION TRACKING

Real-Life MCT Application Log:

Situation: _____

Date/Time: _____

Techniques used:

☐ Attention training principles

☐ Worry postponement

☐ Detached mindfulness

☐ Belief challenging

☐ Other: _____

Effectiveness (1-10): ___

What worked well:
_____

What to try differently next time:
_____

Overall learning from this situation:
_____

Appendix B: Worksheets and Exercises

These worksheets provide structured approaches for implementing MCT concepts and tracking your progress. Unlike general therapy worksheets, these focus specifically on metacognitive processes and attention training rather than thought content analysis.

Metacognitive Beliefs Questionnaire

This assessment helps you identify the specific beliefs about thinking that maintain your anxiety, worry, or depression. Understanding your personal metacognitive profile allows you to customize MCT techniques for maximum effectiveness.

POSITIVE BELIEFS ABOUT WORRY

Rate each statement from 1 (strongly disagree) to 5 (strongly agree):

Worry as Preparation:

- Worrying helps me prepare for problems: 1 2 3 4 5
- If I worry about something, I'll be better able to handle it: 1 2 3 4 5
- Worrying about problems shows that I'm responsible: 1 2 3 4 5
- People who don't worry enough get caught off guard: 1 2 3 4 5

Worry as Care:

- Worrying about people I love shows that I care about them: 1 2 3 4 5

- If I stopped worrying about my family, it would mean I don't love them: 1 2 3 4 5

- Good parents/partners/friends worry about their loved ones: 1 2 3 4 5

- Not worrying about important things would be selfish: 1 2 3 4 5

Worry as Problem-Solving:

- Worrying helps me solve problems: 1 2 3 4 5

- If I think about problems enough, I'll find solutions: 1 2 3 4 5

- Worrying prevents me from making mistakes: 1 2 3 4 5

- I need to worry to make good decisions: 1 2 3 4 5

NEGATIVE BELIEFS ABOUT THINKING

Uncontrollability:

- I have no control over my worry: 1 2 3 4 5

- Once I start worrying, I can't stop: 1 2 3 4 5

- My thoughts control me more than I control them: 1 2 3 4 5

- Worry attacks me randomly without warning: 1 2 3 4 5

Danger of Thoughts:

- Some thoughts are dangerous and must be stopped: 1 2 3 4 5

- Having certain thoughts means something bad about me: 1 2 3 4 5

- If I think about bad things, they're more likely to happen: 1 2 3 4 5

- I must analyze my thoughts to understand what they mean: 1 2 3 4 5

Consequences of Not Thinking:

- If I don't ruminate about problems, I won't understand myself: 1 2 3 4 5
- Stopping worry means I don't care enough: 1 2 3 4 5
- Not thinking about problems is irresponsible: 1 2 3 4 5
- I'll miss important insights if I don't analyze my thoughts: 1 2 3 4 5

SCORING AND INTERPRETATION:

Positive Beliefs Total: ___/60

- 45-60: Strong positive beliefs maintaining worry patterns
- 30-44: Moderate positive beliefs requiring attention
- 15-29: Mild positive beliefs, easily modifiable
- Below 15: Positive beliefs not significantly maintaining patterns

Negative Beliefs Total: ___/60

- 45-60: Strong negative beliefs creating helplessness about thought control
- 30-44: Moderate negative beliefs limiting confidence in change
- 15-29: Mild negative beliefs, good foundation for technique learning
- Below 15: Negative beliefs not significantly blocking progress

Personalized Focus Areas: Based on your scores, prioritize belief challenging work:

- **High positive beliefs:** Focus on behavioral experiments showing worry doesn't actually help
- **High negative beliefs:** Emphasize attention training to build confidence in thought control
- **High both:** Begin with attention training, then add belief challenging gradually

CAS Identification Worksheet

The Cognitive Attentional Syndrome (CAS) manifests differently for each person. This worksheet helps you map your personal CAS pattern, making MCT techniques more targeted and effective.

WORRY COMPONENT ANALYSIS

Worry Triggers: List the top 5 situations, thoughts, or events that typically start your worry cycles:

1. _____
2. _____
3. _____
4. _____
5. _____

Worry Content Themes: Check all categories that capture your typical worry content: ☐ Health (your own or others') ☐ Financial security ☐ Work performance and career ☐ Relationship problems ☐ Family safety and wellbeing ☐ Future catastrophes ☐ Past mistakes and regrets ☐ Social acceptance and rejection ☐ Control and unpredictability ☐ Meaning and life purpose

Worry Timing Patterns: When do you typically experience worry episodes? ☐ Upon waking ☐ During work hours ☐ Evening/before bed ☐ During transitions (travel, schedule changes) ☐ During unstructured time ☐ After positive events (anticipating problems) ☐ After negative events (analyzing what went wrong)

RUMINATION COMPONENT ANALYSIS

Rumination Focus Areas: What do you typically ruminate about? (Check all that apply) ☐ Past mistakes and failures ☐ "Why" questions about problems ☐ Comparing yourself to others ☐ Analyzing your emotions and mental state ☐ Relationship problems and interactions ☐ Unfairness and injustice ☐ Lost opportunities and regrets ☐ Personal inadequacies and flaws

Rumination Triggers: What situations typically start rumination episodes? ☐ Criticism or perceived rejection ☐ Reminders of past failures ☐ Seeing others succeed ☐ Unstructured time alone ☐ Anniversary dates of difficult events ☐ Social media browsing ☐ News consumption ☐ Physical illness or fatigue

ATTENTION CONTROL ASSESSMENT

Current Attention Flexibility: Rate your current ability (1-5 scale, where 1=very difficult, 5=very easy):

- Focusing on conversations without mind wandering: 1 2 3 4 5
- Concentrating on work tasks without distraction: 1 2 3 4 5
- Enjoying activities without analyzing your enjoyment: 1 2 3 4 5
- Listening to others without planning your response: 1 2 3 4 5
- Staying present during pleasant experiences: 1 2 3 4 5

Attention Trap Identification: Where does your attention get "stuck" most often? ☐ Monitoring physical sensations ☐ Analyzing social interactions ☐ Checking for potential threats ☐ Reviewing past events ☐ Predicting future problems ☐ Monitoring your own mood/mental state ☐ Comparing yourself to others ☐ Seeking certainty about uncertain situations

METACOGNITIVE BEHAVIOR PATTERNS

Safety Behaviors: What do you do to try to manage worry, anxiety, or depression? ☐ Seek reassurance from others ☐ Research problems online ☐ Make excessive plans to feel in control ☐ Avoid situations that trigger worry ☐ Check and recheck things ☐ Monitor physical sensations ☐ Analyze past events repeatedly ☐ Seek certainty before making decisions

CAS PATTERN SUMMARY: Based on your responses, your primary CAS pattern appears to be: ☐ Worry-dominant (future-focused anxiety) ☐ Rumination-dominant (past-focused analysis) ☐ Attention-monitoring dominant (self-focused surveillance) ☐ Mixed pattern (combination of multiple elements)

Priority Technique Focus: Based on your CAS pattern, prioritize these MCT techniques:

- Worry-dominant: Worry postponement + attention training
- Rumination-dominant: Rumination interruption + future-focused attention
- Attention-monitoring: External attention training + detached mindfulness
- Mixed pattern: Begin with attention training, then add other techniques gradually

Weekly Practice Logs

Consistent practice tracking helps maintain motivation while identifying patterns in your MCT skill development. These logs focus on practice completion and technique effectiveness rather than mood monitoring.

WEEKLY MCT PRACTICE RECORD

Week Starting: _____

Daily Attention Training:

	Completed?	Duration	Focus Quality (1-10)	Notes
Mon:	Y / N	___min	_____	_____
Tue:	Y / N	___min	_____	_____
Wed:	Y / N	___min	_____	_____
Thu:	Y / N	___min	_____	_____
Fri:	Y / N	___min	_____	_____
Sat:	Y / N	___min	_____	_____
Sun:	Y / N	___min	_____	_____

Worry Postponement Practice:

	Attempts	Successes	Most Challenging Situation
Mon:	____	____	_____
Tue:	____	____	_____
Wed:	____	____	_____
Thu:	____	____	_____
Fri:	____	____	_____
Sat:	____	____	_____

Sun: ____ ____ _____

Detached Mindfulness Applications: Record situations where you successfully used detached mindfulness:

Situation 1: _____ **Technique used:** _____ **Effectiveness (1-10):** ____

Situation 2: _____ **Technique used:** _____ **Effectiveness (1-10):** ____

Situation 3: _____ **Technique used:** _____ **Effectiveness (1-10):** ____

Weekly Reflection Questions:

1. Which technique felt most natural this week?
2. What situation challenged your MCT skills most?
3. What improvement did you notice in your thinking patterns?
4. What do you want to focus on practicing next week?

Behavioral Experiment Templates

Behavioral experiments test whether your beliefs about worry, rumination, and attention control are actually accurate. These structured experiments provide evidence for developing healthier metacognitive beliefs.

WORRY EFFECTIVENESS EXPERIMENT

Belief to Test: "Worrying about [specific topic] helps me prepare and prevents problems"

Experiment Design:

- **Week 1:** Worry about the chosen topic as much as usual
- **Week 2:** Postpone all worry about this topic using MCT techniques
- **Week 3:** Return to normal worry patterns

Tracking Measures:

- Problem-solving actions taken each week
- Actual negative outcomes related to this topic
- Stress levels related to this topic (1-10 daily)
- Time spent thinking about this topic
- Quality of decisions made about this topic

Week 1 (Normal Worry) Results:

- Actions taken: _____
- Problems that occurred: _____
- Average stress level: ___
- Time spent worrying: ___ minutes/day
- Decision quality: ___

Week 2 (Worry Postponement) Results:

- Actions taken: _____
- Problems that occurred: _____
- Average stress level: ___
- Time spent worrying: ___ minutes/day
- Decision quality: ___

Week 3 (Return to Normal) Results:

- Actions taken: _____
- Problems that occurred: _____
- Average stress level: ___
- Time spent worrying: ___ minutes/day
- Decision quality: ___

Conclusions:

- Did worry actually help with preparation? Y/N
- Did worry prevent any actual problems? Y/N
- Did worry improve or worsen your stress levels?
- What does this tell you about the usefulness of worry for this topic?

THOUGHT CONTROL EXPERIMENT

Belief to Test: "I can't control my thoughts" or "Once worry starts, I can't stop it"

Experiment 1 - Attention Flexibility:

- **Day 1-2:** Try to think about a white elephant for 5 minutes straight
- **Day 3-4:** Try NOT to think about a white elephant for 5 minutes
- **Day 5-6:** Practice switching attention between white elephant and blue elephant every 30 seconds
- **Day 7:** Practice noticing white elephant thoughts without engaging with them

Results: What did you learn about your ability to direct and control attention?

Experiment 2 - Worry Control:

- **Phase 1:** Next time worry starts, set a timer for 10 minutes and worry intensively

- **Phase 2:** After 10 minutes, use attention training to redirect focus externally

- **Phase 3:** Notice whether you can influence worry duration and intensity

Results: What evidence did you gather about your ability to influence worry patterns?

RUMINATION USEFULNESS EXPERIMENT

Belief to Test: "Ruminating about my problems helps me understand myself and find solutions"

Two-Week Comparison:

- **Week A:** Ruminate about chosen problem as much as feels natural

- **Week B:** Limit rumination to 15 minutes daily during scheduled time

Tracking:

	Week A (Unlimited)	Week B (Limited)
Insights gained:	_____	_____
Solutions found:	_____	_____
Actions taken:	_____	_____
Mood (avg 1-10):	_____	_____
Problem severity:	_____	_____

Analysis Questions:

- Did unlimited rumination lead to more insights than limited rumination?
- Which week resulted in more problem-solving actions?
- Which approach left you feeling better overall?
- What does this suggest about rumination's actual usefulness?

Relapse Prevention Planning Sheets

Maintaining MCT gains requires preparation for situations that might trigger return to old metacognitive patterns. These planning sheets help you identify risk factors and develop specific response strategies.

PERSONAL RELAPSE RISK ASSESSMENT

High-Risk Situations: Identify situations most likely to trigger return to old worry/rumination patterns:

Stress-Based Triggers: ☐ Work deadlines and pressure ☐ Relationship conflicts ☐ Health concerns (self or family) ☐ Financial stress ☐ Major life changes ☐ Anniversary dates of difficult events ☐ Family gatherings or holidays ☐ Travel and schedule disruptions

Internal State Triggers: ☐ Physical illness or fatigue ☐ Hormonal changes ☐ Sleep disruption ☐ Alcohol or substance use ☐ Depression episodes ☐ High anxiety periods ☐ Social isolation ☐ Boredom or lack of structure

EARLY WARNING SIGN RECOGNITION

Attention Pattern Changes:

- Increased self-monitoring or symptom checking
- Difficulty concentrating during conversations
- Mind wandering during previously enjoyable activities

- Increased social comparison and monitoring
- Return to excessive news or social media consumption

Metacognitive Pattern Changes:
- Increased "what if" thinking
- Return to past-event analysis
- Seeking excessive reassurance
- Making plans to prevent unlikely problems
- Increased second-guessing of decisions

Behavioral Pattern Changes:
- Avoiding situations that previously felt manageable
- Returning to safety behaviors
- Increased research about problems or symptoms
- Seeking certainty before making routine decisions
- Postponing activities due to worry

INTERVENTION STRATEGIES

Immediate Response Protocol: When you notice early warning signs:

1. **Acknowledge:** "I notice I'm returning to old patterns"
2. **Assess:** "What triggered this change?"
3. **Apply:** "Which MCT technique should I use right now?"
4. **Act:** Implement chosen technique immediately
5. **Adjust:** Increase MCT practice intensity temporarily

Intensive Practice Period:

- Double attention training frequency (twice daily)
- Return to strict worry postponement
- Increase external attention activities
- Limit rumination triggers (news, social media, certain conversations)
- Schedule daily check-ins with MCT technique application

Support Activation:

- Contact MCT-informed friends or family
- Schedule appointment with MCT therapist if available
- Increase structured social activities
- Join online MCT support communities
- Consider temporary increase in self-care activities

Recovery Timeline Expectations:

- **Days 1-3:** Recognize patterns and implement intensive practice
- **Week 1:** Notice some improvement in attention control
- **Weeks 2-3:** Return to previous MCT skill levels
- **Week 4+:** Integrate lessons learned from relapse experience

Long-Term Prevention Strategies:

- Maintain minimum daily attention training practice
- Regular metacognitive belief review (monthly)
- Ongoing application of MCT principles in daily situations
- Annual MCT skill refresher (re-read key chapters)

- Environmental design supporting metacognitive health

Appendix C: Additional Resources

These resources extend your MCT learning beyond this book's scope. Whether you want deeper scientific understanding, community support, or professional training opportunities, these carefully selected resources provide authentic, high-quality information about metacognitive therapy.

Recommended Further Reading

FOUNDATIONAL MCT TEXTS

Wells, A. (2009). *Metacognitive therapy for anxiety and depression.* **Guilford Press.** The definitive professional text on MCT theory and practice. While written for therapists, motivated readers will find detailed explanations of metacognitive assessment and treatment protocols. This book provides the complete scientific foundation underlying the techniques in this self-help guide.

Wells, A. (2000). *Emotional disorders and metacognition: Innovative cognitive therapy.* **Wiley.** Wells' original presentation of metacognitive theory. More theoretical than the 2009 text but excellent for understanding how MCT differs from other cognitive approaches. Includes early research findings that established MCT as a distinct therapeutic method.

Wells, A., & Matthews, G. (1994). *Attention and emotion: A clinical perspective.* **Erlbaum.** The foundational text explaining the relationship between attention processes and emotional disorders. Provides scientific background for understanding why attention training is so effective for anxiety and depression.

PRACTICAL APPLICATION GUIDES

Normann, N., & Morina, N. (2018). *The efficacy of metacognitive therapy: A systematic review and meta-analysis.* **Frontiers in Psychology, 9, 2211.** Comprehensive review of MCT research across different anxiety and depression disorders. Excellent for understanding the scientific evidence supporting MCT effectiveness compared to other treatment approaches.

Spada, M. M., Mohiyeddini, C., & Wells, A. (2008). *Measuring metacognitions associated with emotional distress: Factor structure and predictive validity of the metacognitions questionnaire-30.* **Personality and Individual Differences, 45(3), 238-242.** Technical paper describing metacognitive belief assessment. Useful for readers wanting to understand the research foundation for metacognitive belief identification and modification.

SPECIALIZED APPLICATIONS

Papageorgiou, C., & Wells, A. (Eds.). (2004). *Depressive rumination: Nature, theory and treatment.* **Wiley.** Comprehensive examination of rumination in depression with MCT treatment approaches. Essential reading for understanding how MCT specifically addresses depressive thinking patterns.

Fisher, P., & Wells, A. (2009). *Metacognitive therapy for obsessive-compulsive disorder: A case series.* **Journal of Behavior Therapy and Experimental Psychiatry, 40(1), 117-132.** Detailed case studies showing MCT application for OCD. Demonstrates how metacognitive approaches address obsessions and compulsions differently than traditional exposure-based treatments.

Online Communities and Support Groups

PROFESSIONAL MCT COMMUNITIES

International Association for Metacognitive Therapy (IAMCT) Website: www.iamct.org The primary professional organization for MCT practitioners and researchers. Offers conference information, research updates, and practitioner directories. While focused on professionals, the public resources section provides excellent MCT information for general audiences.

MCT Institute Forums Online discussion forums moderated by MCT-trained professionals. These communities provide peer support for people learning MCT techniques while maintaining scientific accuracy in discussions about technique application.

GENERAL SUPPORT COMMUNITIES

Reddit Metacognitive Therapy Community Active community of people practicing MCT techniques with moderated discussions about technique application, progress sharing, and troubleshooting common challenges. Good source for peer support and practical advice.

Facebook Metacognitive Therapy Support Groups Several private Facebook groups focus on MCT practice and support. These groups require admin approval and maintain guidelines about appropriate sharing of personal information while providing community connection.

CRISIS SUPPORT RESOURCES

National Suicide Prevention Lifeline: 988 24/7 crisis support for people experiencing suicidal thoughts or severe mental health crises. Trained counselors familiar with various therapy approaches including cognitive and metacognitive techniques.

Crisis Text Line: Text HOME to 741741 Text-based crisis support available 24/7. Particularly useful for people who prefer written communication during crisis situations.

NAMI (National Alliance on Mental Illness) Website: www.nami.org Provides education, support groups, and advocacy for mental health. Local NAMI chapters often offer support groups that welcome people using various therapeutic approaches including MCT.

Professional Training Information

MCT CERTIFICATION PROGRAMS

Adrian Wells MCT Training (Greater Manchester, UK) The original and most authoritative MCT training program, conducted by MCT's developer. Offers basic and advanced certification for mental health professionals. Training includes theoretical foundations, assessment methods, and supervised practice.

MCT Institute International Training Provides MCT training programs in multiple countries with standardized curricula based on Wells' original training model. Offers both in-person and online training options for qualified mental health professionals.

TRAINING PREREQUISITES MCT professional training typically requires:

- Licensed mental health professional status (psychology, counseling, social work, psychiatry)
- Basic cognitive therapy training and experience
- Commitment to supervised practice and certification requirements
- Continuing education maintenance for certification renewal

TRAINING COMPONENTS

- **Theoretical foundations:** Metacognitive model, CAS theory, attention regulation
- **Assessment skills:** Metacognitive belief identification, CAS pattern recognition

- **Technique training:** Attention training, detached mindfulness, worry postponement
- **Case formulation:** Developing individualized MCT treatment plans
- **Supervision requirements:** Supervised practice with feedback and skill refinement

CONTINUING EDUCATION

- Annual MCT conferences with research updates and advanced technique training
- Online webinar series for certified practitioners
- Research collaboration opportunities
- Advanced specialty training (trauma, OCD, depression applications)

Research References for the Curious

For readers interested in the scientific foundations underlying MCT techniques, these research papers provide detailed evidence for MCT effectiveness and theoretical development.

META-ANALYSES AND SYSTEMATIC REVIEWS

Normann, N., & Morina, N. (2018). The efficacy of metacognitive therapy for anxiety and depression: A meta-analytic review. *Frontiers in Psychology*, **9, 2211.** Comprehensive analysis of MCT outcome studies showing superior effectiveness compared to CBT and other treatments across anxiety and depressive disorders.

Capobianco, L., Faija, C., Husain, Z., & Wells, A. (2020). Metacognitive therapy for anxiety and depression: A systematic review and meta-analysis. *Journal of Anxiety Disorders*, **76,**

102323. Recent meta-analysis confirming MCT effectiveness with updated research including larger sample sizes and longer follow-up periods.

FOUNDATIONAL RESEARCH STUDIES

Wells, A., Welford, M., King, P., Papageorgiou, C., Wisely, J., & Mendel, E. (2010). A pilot randomized trial of metacognitive therapy vs applied relaxation in the treatment of adults with generalized anxiety disorder. *Behaviour Research and Therapy*, **48(5), 429-434.** Landmark study establishing MCT superiority over relaxation training for generalized anxiety disorder.

Wells, A., & King, P. (2006). Metacognitive therapy for generalized anxiety disorder: An open trial. *Journal of Behavior Therapy and Experimental Psychiatry*, **37(3), 206-212.** Early clinical trial demonstrating MCT effectiveness for GAD with detailed case examples and outcome measures.

ATTENTION TRAINING RESEARCH

Fergus, T. A., & Bardeen, J. R. (2016). The attention training technique causally reduces self-focus following worry induction: Evidence from a laboratory study. *Behaviour Research and Therapy*, **81, 46-53.** Controlled laboratory study showing that attention training directly reduces problematic self-focused attention following worry induction.

Knowles, M. M., Foden, P., El-Deredy, W., & Wells, A. (2016). A systematic review of efficacy of the attention training technique in clinical and nonclinical samples. *Journal of Clinical Psychology*, **72(10), 999-1025.** Systematic review of attention training research across multiple populations and conditions, demonstrating broad applicability of attention control training.

Audio Resources and Apps

GUIDED ATTENTION TRAINING RECORDINGS

Official MCT Audio Programs The MCT Institute produces professional attention training recordings narrated by certified MCT practitioners. These recordings provide standardized ATT guidance with appropriate timing and instruction quality.

Attention Training Apps Several smartphone apps provide structured attention training programs based on MCT principles. Look for apps specifically mentioning metacognitive therapy rather than general mindfulness apps, as the focus and techniques differ significantly.

PODCAST RESOURCES

"The Metacognitive Therapy Podcast" Regular episodes featuring MCT practitioners discussing technique applications, research updates, and case examples. Episodes range from beginner-friendly explanations to advanced clinical discussions.

Mental health podcasts featuring MCT episodes: Many general mental health podcasts occasionally feature episodes about MCT. These provide accessible introductions to MCT concepts and real-world application examples.

SELF-RECORDING GUIDELINES

Creating Personal ATT Recordings: You can create personalized attention training recordings:

1. **Script preparation:** Use the ATT instructions from Chapter 4
2. **Recording quality:** Clear audio without background noise
3. **Timing precision:** Exact timing for each phase (4 minutes each)

4. **Voice tone:** Calm, clear instruction without excessive emotion

5. **Personal customization:** Include sounds specific to your environment

Recording Equipment:

- Smartphone voice recording apps provide adequate quality
- External microphones improve sound quality if desired
- Test recordings for clarity and appropriate volume levels
- Create multiple versions for different practice preferences

MEDITATION AND MINDFULNESS APPS WITH MCT COMPATIBILITY

While MCT differs from traditional mindfulness, some meditation apps provide features compatible with MCT practice:

Apps with attention training elements:

- Look for programs focusing on attention flexibility rather than relaxation
- Choose guided sessions emphasizing external attention rather than internal monitoring
- Avoid apps that encourage extensive self-analysis or emotional processing
- Select programs teaching attention control skills rather than just stress reduction

Customizing meditation apps for MCT:

- Use attention-based meditations, skip emotion-focused sessions

- Practice external attention focus during mindfulness exercises
- Apply detached mindfulness principles to meditation content
- Avoid getting trapped in meditation performance monitoring

Creating Your MCT Resource Library

Build a personalized collection of MCT resources that supports your ongoing practice and continued learning:

Essential Daily Resources:

- Technique cheat sheets (printed or on phone)
- Progress tracking templates
- Emergency protocol cards
- Attention training audio recordings

Weekly Resources:

- Practice logs and behavioral experiment templates
- Metacognitive belief assessment tools
- Relapse prevention planning materials
- Community support contact information

Ongoing Learning Resources:

- Research paper bookmarks for deeper understanding
- Professional training information for future consideration
- Book recommendations for continued education
- Conference and workshop notifications

Building Your Support Network:

- Contact information for MCT-informed professionals
- Friends and family members who understand your MCT practice
- Online community memberships
- Crisis support resources

Technology Integration:

- Calendar reminders for daily practice
- Note-taking apps for technique application tracking
- Audio recording capabilities for ATT practice
- Bookmarking systems for research and resource access

The goal isn't to collect resources endlessly but to create a practical toolkit that supports your MCT practice and continued growth. Choose resources that enhance your practice rather than creating additional tasks or pressure.

Your MCT journey continues beyond this book. These resources provide the support, community, and continued learning opportunities that help maintain your progress and deepen your skills over time. The techniques you've learned become more powerful and automatic with ongoing practice and community support.

The most important resource, however, is your own experience with MCT techniques. Trust what you learn through practice, notice what works best for your specific situations, and continue refining your approach based on real-world results rather than theoretical perfection.

Reference

- Anderson, M. C., & Green, C. (2001). Suppressing unwanted memories by executive control. *Nature, 410*(6826), 366–369.

- Barsky, A. J., & Ahern, D. K. (2004). Cognitive behavior therapy for hypochondriasis: A randomized controlled trial. *JAMA, 291*(12), 1464–1470. https://doi.org/10.1001/jama.291.12.1464

- Bergström, Z. M., de Fockert, J. W., & Richardson-Klavehn, A. (2009). ERP and behavioural evidence for direct suppression of unwanted memories. *NeuroImage, 48*(4), 726–737.

- Bishop, S. R., Lau, M., Shapiro, S., Carlson, L., Anderson, N. D., Carmody, J., Segal, Z. V., Abbey, S., Speca, M., Velting, D., & Devins, G. (2004). Mindfulness: A proposed operational definition. *Clinical Psychology: Science and Practice, 11*(3), 230–241. https://doi.org/10.1093/clipsy.bph077

- Borkovec, T. D., Robinson, E., Pruzinsky, T., & DePree, J. A. (1983). Preliminary exploration of worry: Some characteristics and processes. *Behaviour Research and Therapy, 21*(1), 9–16. https://doi.org/10.1016/0005-7967(83)90121-3

- Brewer, J. A., Worhunsky, P. D., Gray, J. R., Tang, Y. Y., Weber, J., & Kober, H. (2011). Meditation experience is associated with differences in default mode network activity and connectivity. *Proceedings of the National Academy of Sciences, 108*(50), 20254–20259.

- Butler, A. C., Chapman, J. E., Forman, E. M., & Beck, A. T. (2006). The empirical status of cognitive-behavioral therapy:

A review of meta-analyses. *Clinical Psychology Review, 26*(1), 17–31.

- Callinan, S., Johnson, D., & Wells, A. (2015). A randomised controlled study of the effects of the attention training technique on traumatic stress symptoms, emotional attention set shifting, and flexibility. *Cognitive Therapy and Research, 39*(1), 4–13.

- Capobianco, L., & Nordahl, H. M. (2023). A brief history of metacognitive therapy: From cognitive science to clinical practice. *Cognitive and Behavioral Practice, 30*(1), 45–54. https://doi.org/10.1016/j.cbpra.2021.11.002

- Capobianco, L., Faija, C., Husain, Z., & Wells, A. (2018). Metacognitive beliefs and their relationship with anxiety and depression in physical illnesses: A systematic review. *PLOS ONE, 13*(7), e0199822.

- Clark, D. M., & Wells, A. (1995). A cognitive model of social phobia. In R. G. Heimberg, M. R. Liebowitz, D. A. Hope, & F. R. Schneier (Eds.), *Social phobia: Diagnosis, assessment, and treatment* (pp. 69–93). Guilford Press.

- Clark, D. M., Ball, S., & Pape, D. (1991). An experimental investigation of thought suppression. *Behaviour Research and Therapy, 29*(3), 253–257.

- Fergus, T. A., & Bardeen, J. R. (2013). The attention training technique causally reduces self-focus following worry induction: A comparison of brief interventions. *Cognitive Therapy and Research, 37*(6), 1291–1295.

- Fergus, T. A., & Bardeen, J. R. (2016). The attention training technique: A review of a neurobehavioral therapy for emotional disorders. *Cognitive and Behavioral Practice, 23*(4), 502–516.

- Fergus, T. A., Wheless, N. E., & Wright, L. C. (2014). The attention training technique, self-focused attention, and anxiety: A laboratory-based component study. *Behaviour Research and Therapy, 61*, 150–155.

- Franklin, M. E., & Foa, E. B. (2007). Cognitive behavioral treatment of obsessive-compulsive disorder. In P. E. Nathan & J. M. Gorman (Eds.), *A guide to treatments that work* (3rd ed., pp. 431–446). Oxford University Press.

- Gross, J. J. (2015). Emotion regulation: Current status and future prospects. *Psychological Inquiry, 26*(1), 1–26.

- Hagen, R., Hjemdal, O., Solem, S., Kennair, L. E. O., Nordahl, H. M., Fisher, P., & Wells, A. (2017). Metacognitive therapy for depression in adults: A waiting list randomized controlled trial with six months follow-up. *Frontiers in Psychology, 8*, 31.

- Halvorsen, M., Hagen, R., Hjemdal, O., Eriksen, M. S., Sørli, Å. J., Waterloo, K., ... Solem, S. (2015). Metacognitive therapy for depression: A 6-month follow-up. *Frontiers in Psychology, 6*, 1315.

- Hjemdal, O., Solem, S., Hagen, R., Kennair, L. E. O., Nordahl, H. M., & Wells, A. (2019). A randomized controlled trial of metacognitive therapy for depression: Analysis of 1-year follow-up. *Frontiers in Psychology, 10*, 1842.

- Hollon, S. D., DeRubeis, R. J., Shelton, R. C., Amsterdam, J. D., Salomon, R. M., O'Reardon, J. P., ... Gallop, R. (2005). Prevention of relapse following cognitive therapy vs medications in moderate to severe depression. *Archives of General Psychiatry, 62*(4), 417–422.

- Johnson, S. U., Hoffart, A., Nordahl, H. M., & Wampold, B. E. (2017). Metacognitive therapy versus disorder-specific CBT for comorbid anxiety disorders: A randomized controlled trial. *Journal of Anxiety Disorders, 50*, 103–112.

- Knowles, M. M., Foden, P., El-Deredy, W., & Wells, A. (2016). A systematic review of efficacy of the attention training technique in clinical and nonclinical samples. *Journal of Clinical Psychology, 72*(10), 999–1025.

- Kowalski, J., Wierzba, M., Wypych, M., Marchewka, A., & Dragan, M. (2020). Effects of the attention training technique on brain function in high- and low-cognitive-attentional syndrome individuals: Regional dynamics before, during, and after a single session of ATT. *Behaviour Research and Therapy, 132,* 103693. https://doi.org/10.1016/j.brat.2020.103693

- Najmi, S., & Wegner, D. M. (2008). The gravity of unwanted thoughts: Asymmetric priming effects in thought suppression. *Consciousness and Cognition, 17*(1), 114–124.

- Nolen-Hoeksema, S. (2000). The role of rumination in depressive disorders and mixed anxiety/depressive symptoms. *Journal of Abnormal Psychology, 109*(3), 504–511.

- Nolen-Hoeksema, S., Wisco, B. E., & Lyubomirsky, S. (2008). Rethinking rumination. *Perspectives on Psychological Science, 3*(5), 400–424.

- Nordahl, H., & Wells, A. (2017). Testing the metacognitive model against the benchmark CBT model of social anxiety disorder: Is it time to move beyond cognition? *PLOS ONE, 12*(5), e0177109.

- Nordahl, H., Nordahl, H. M., Hjemdal, O., & Wells, A. (2019). Cognitive and metacognitive predictors of symptom improvement following treatment of social anxiety disorder: A secondary analysis from a randomized controlled trial. *Clinical Psychology & Psychotherapy, 26*(2), 197–208.

- Nordahl, H. M., Borkovec, T. D., Hagen, R., Kennair, L. E. O., Hjemdal, O., Solem, S., … Wells, A. (2018). Metacognitive therapy versus cognitive–behavioural therapy

- in adults with generalised anxiety disorder. *BJPsych Open, 4*(5), 393–400.

- Normann, N., & Morina, N. (2018). The efficacy of metacognitive therapy: A systematic review and meta-analysis. *Frontiers in Psychology, 9*, 2211.

- Papageorgiou, C., & Wells, A. (2000). Treatment of recurrent major depression with attention training. *Cognitive and Behavioral Practice, 7*(4), 407–413.

- Papageorgiou, C., & Wells, A. (2003). An empirical test of a clinical metacognitive model of rumination and depression. *Cognitive Therapy and Research, 27*(3), 261–273.

- Purdon, C., & Clark, D. A. (2001). Suppression of obsession-like thoughts in nonclinical individuals: Impact on thought frequency, appraisal and mood state. *Behaviour Research and Therapy, 39*(10), 1163–1181.

- Rachman, S., & De Silva, P. (1978). Abnormal and normal obsessions. *Behaviour Research and Therapy, 16*(4), 233–248.

- Sibrava, N. J., Bjornsson, A. S., Pérez Benítez, A. C. I., Moitra, E., Weisberg, R. B., & Keller, M. B. (2019). Posttraumatic stress disorder in African American and Latinx adults: Clinical course and the role of racial and ethnic discrimination. *American Psychologist, 74*(1), 101–116.

- Siegle, G. J., Ghinassi, F., & Thase, M. E. (2007). Neurobehavioral therapies in the 21st century: Summary of an emerging field and an extended example of cognitive control training for depression. *Cognitive Therapy and Research, 31*(2), 235–262.

- Solem, S., Kennair, L. E. O., Hagen, R., Havnen, A., Nordahl, H. M., Wells, A., & Hjemdal, O. (2019). Metacognitive therapy for depression: A 3-year follow-up study assessing

- recovery, relapse, work force participation, and quality of life. *Frontiers in Psychology, 10*, 2908.
- Spada, M. M., Caselli, G., Nikčević, A. V., & Wells, A. (2015). Metacognition in addictive behaviors. *Addictive Behaviors, 44*, 9–15. https://doi.org/10.1016/j.addbeh.2014.08.002
- Spada, M. M., Mohiyeddini, C., & Wells, A. (2008). Measuring metacognitions associated with emotional distress: Factor structure and predictive validity of the metacognitions questionnaire 30. *Personality and Individual Differences, 45*(3), 238–242.
- Wegner, D. M. (1994). Ironic processes of mental control. *Psychological Review, 101*(1), 34–52.
- Wegner, D. M., & Erber, R. (1992). The hyperaccessibility of suppressed thoughts. *Journal of Personality and Social Psychology, 63*(6), 903–912.
- Wegner, D. M., Schneider, D. J., Carter, S. R., & White, T. L. (1987). Paradoxical effects of thought suppression. *Journal of Personality and Social Psychology, 53*(1), 5–13.
- Wells, A. (1990). Panic disorder in association with relaxation-induced anxiety: An attentional training approach to treatment. *Behavior Therapy, 21*(3), 273–280.
- Wells, A. (2009). *Metacognitive therapy for anxiety and depression*. Guilford Press.
- Wells, A., & Carter, K. (2001). Further tests of a cognitive model of generalized anxiety disorder: Metacognitions and worry in GAD, panic disorder, social phobia, depression, and nonpatients. *Behavior Therapy, 32*(1), 85–102.
- Wells, A., & Colbear, J. S. (2012). Treating posttraumatic stress disorder with metacognitive therapy: A preliminary controlled trial. *Journal of Clinical Psychology, 68*(4), 373–381. https://doi.org/10.1002/jclp.20871

- Wells, A., & Matthews, G. (1994). *Attention and emotion: A clinical perspective*. Lawrence Erlbaum Associates.
- Wells, A., & Matthews, G. (2015). *Attention and emotion: A clinical perspective* (2nd ed.). Psychology Press.
- Wells, A., & Papageorgiou, C. (2001). Brief cognitive therapy for social phobia: A case series. *Behaviour Research and Therapy, 39*(6), 713–720.
- Wells, A., Welford, M., King, P., Papageorgiou, C., Wisely, J., & Mendel, E. (2010). A pilot randomized trial of metacognitive therapy vs applied relaxation in the treatment of adults with generalized anxiety disorder. *Behaviour Research and Therapy, 48*(5), 429–434. https://doi.org/10.1016/j.brat.2009.11.013
- Wells, A., Fisher, P., Myers, S., Wheatley, J., Patel, T., & Brewin, C. R. (2012). Metacognitive therapy in treatment-resistant depression: A platform trial. *Behaviour Research and Therapy, 50*(6), 367–373. https://doi.org/10.1016/j.brat.2012.02.004
- Wells, A., Walton, D., Lovell, K., & Proctor, D. (2015). Metacognitive therapy versus prolonged exposure in adults with chronic post-traumatic stress disorder: A parallel randomized controlled trial. *Cognitive Therapy and Research, 39*(1), 70–80. https://doi.org/10.1007/s10608-014-9636-6
- Wenzlaff, R. M., & Wegner, D. M. (2000). Thought suppression. *Annual Review of Psychology, 51*(1), 59–91.
- Yilmaz, A. E., Gençöz, T., & Wells, A. (2011). The temporal precedence of metacognition in the development of anxiety and depression symptoms in the context of life-stress: A prospective study. *Journal of Anxiety Disorders, 25*(3), 389–396. https://doi.org/10.1016/j.janxdis.2010.11.001

www.ingramcontent.com/pod-product-compliance
Lightning Source LLC
Chambersburg PA
CBHW062155080426
42734CB00010B/1701